BUILD
AND
GROW

How to go from Tradesperson to Managing Director
in the Construction and Trade Industries

ALISON WARNER

RETHINK PRESS

First published in Great Britain 2017
by Rethink Press (www.rethinkpress.com)

© Copyright Alison Warner

Cover image © Shutterstock / mihalec

CONTENTS

For all those business owners with untapped potential

FOREWORD

Make some room, you have a new tool to slot into your kit. This book you're holding – it's got all the nuts to tighten your business plan, and the bolts to secure effective systems and processes. Blimey, I could have done with this when I first started out.

'When I first started out' – now that's something I've been asked about thousands of times! But the story still feels fresh when I see the reactions on the faces of people who ask me about my journey.

Alison was no exception. Sitting in my office discussing my rise from a one-man band to a multimillion pound company, she asked with intrigue, 'How did you come off the tools?' And my reply? It was the hardest, yet most important part of my journey.

Coming off the tools was no easy feat. The only way to describe it... feeling like a tiger in a cage.

I mean why do I, a plumber who relies on tools not computers, need an office? I'm sure many of you are still trying to juggle running your business and the odd job all by yourself – but let me ask you, how effective and efficient are you being with your time?

Time is a scarce resource and I always say if I could do things differently I would have come off the tools sooner. Why? It is what enabled me to build and grow my business.

Putting down the plunger to focus on developing a business that is organised and functional without compromising on quality was top of my agenda, and to do this I needed to be behind a desk, not down a bog.

Alison agreed with me on this, and shocked me with a crazy statistic that 70% of all insolvencies in the UK come from the construction sector. I reckon one of the main reasons that this figure is so high is the fear of trusting others with your business.

I stand by the fact that delegating responsibility is one of the biggest challenges you will face when running a business. Alison addresses this topic in Chapter 5 of this book, taking experience from working in HR for some of the most successful global brands and from her most recent role as a business coach.

She has developed what I think is a clever pathway for coming off the tools to becoming a successful managing director of your own construction and trades business. Using the BUILD system, Alison hits the nail on the head with a formula to transform your business and take it to the next level.

This book isn't just a glimpse behind the curtain; but is a comprehensive collection of advice, case studies and crucial tips on how to elevate your business, as I did mine. At the end of the day, what makes you different from me? We're all tradespeople drinking from the same teapot! The only difference is, I hung up my tools.

Charlie Mullins OBE
Founder and Chairman of Pimlico Plumbers and Author
of *Bog Standard Business*
http://www.pimlicoplumbers.com

PREFACE

At last! Some real sound advice from a true expert in the construction and trade industries, an expert who will actually show you how to make your business grow and work for you from the foundation up.

I have been working in this business alongside tradespeople for nearly twenty years. In this time, I have seen more self-help business books than you could shake a trowel at. I've met with thousands of trades over this time, and there has always been a common theme – trades are experts at their trade, but not necessarily good at 'business'.

That's why I'm finding myself quite excited with this new book. No over the top business language, no jargon to try and unravel.

Alison's book reads like she is right there with you, helping you with every step to make the right decisions so you can find the right way to make your business a success.

With a huge amount of real, hands on business experience, Alison has a wealth of knowledge to share with you. Couple that with her extensive coaching skills and you have the perfect combination of what tools you need and how best to use them to allow your business to grow.

The book provides a simple, easy to follow process of identifying exactly what you need to work on. It shows you how to make the right decisions, the best choices, the dos and don'ts and, more importantly, how to do it yourself.

Some may not think that reading a book is good use of their time, but in this instance they would be wrong – this book is a must! So, put down your tools, start reading and start moving upwards. You'll be so glad you did!

Claire Byrne ACMA, Head of Finance, Checkatrade.com

INTRODUCTION

I had my first business meeting at the age of six… in the dining room at home on a Sunday morning. My dad had his own business, a gardening and hardware shop in the village in which we lived, and one of my earliest memories is of him 'doing his books'. In meticulously neat writing, he recorded all of the takings in large ledgers, transaction by transaction, for each week.

In 1978, all business was conducted via cash or cheque, and Sunday was the day to balance the books. This was how I learnt to budget. I would sit beside him with my own 'ledger', in the form of a small notebook, and my piggy bank. I received the grand sum of 20p pocket money each week and I balanced my books, taking into account anything I had spent in the previous week (which was a rarity).

Once a year we would go on a family holiday to Filey in North Yorkshire (we did this ten years in a run), and the huge sum of £5 would mysteriously appear in the piggy bank, which completely threw my books out.

I think it was clear from the start that I was destined for the business world, as opposed to the more traditional route for girls of marriage and children. I had absolutely no interest in playing Mummies and Daddies with dolls, finding myself much more at home taking an imaginary register of a school class or playing shops.

Why I do what I do

Lacking in confidence was the short sentence that appeared on every single one of my school reports. It was 1982 and I had just finished a pretty horrendous year, caused in the main by a teacher who shouldn't have been allowed near children. I have often wondered why my life has taken the path it has. Someone once said to me that you can only really have empathy with someone's situation if you have been there yourself. Like many of us, I was meant to have a bad experience early in life so that I could empathise with others later on.

Perhaps more crucially, I also have a knack of being able to identify and develop untapped potential in those who don't necessarily push themselves forward. I was not a child who pushed herself forward, and as a consequence perhaps never developed my full potential while at school. This is now what gives me purpose; it is why I do what I do.

When I think back to my early years in management, I often think of one of my first employees. I had recently taken over a a delivery unit of a well known Pizza chain, and was so proud of my little business, determined to make a success of it. But the team needed a lot of direction.

The business began to achieve sales growth of 25% on the previous year within the first few weeks of me taking over, and half the team had had to go in the process. It was imperative that staff were trained in many different tasks so that they were as flexible as possible, hence improving productivity. Tasks included answering the phone, cleaning the oven, etc., but their primary role was to deliver the pizzas. I was 23 and quite black and white in how I managed people in those days – it was my way or the highway, and I wasn't frightened to hire and fire.

This particular employee was no angel; he had been in and out of prison during his life, and he was only 25, but there was something different about him. I saw potential in him, although I wouldn't have necessarily been able to articulate it as such at the time. He was a delivery driver, but I asked him to learn how to answer the phones to take orders within my first few weeks. However, he had other ideas. In his view, he was a driver and nothing more.

Now, normally his refusal to adapt would have resulted in a disciplinary. You could argue that this is what should have happened, but I decided to take a different tack and completely ignored his little outburst. He was testing me, wanting a reaction, so I gave him exactly the opposite.

Approximately two weeks later, he and I were both standing at the front of the store. The phone rang and he picked it up, taking the customer's order right in front of me and operating our fairly complicated computer system at the same time to process it. He had secretly sought out training from someone on the team when I wasn't around, with the sole purpose of surprising me. He had done what I wanted…but on his terms.

He went on to become Head Delivery Driver, responsible for training the staff and looking after the fleet of bikes. When I moved on a year later to another store, I realised he had taught me as much about managing people as any course I had been on, and in some cases more. I often wonder what he is doing now.

I went on to be an Area Manager with the company in a demographically challenging area in North London, where it was absolutely essential to spot talent and develop it. Out of the 11 stores I managed, by the time I moved on, nine had managers who had been developed from entry level positions.

Around the year 2000, I read a book written by the Founder of a new high end coffee chain in the UK. The company had been grown on values very similar to my own, and I was inspired by their philosophy, which centred around finding the right people and treating them well. In turn, they would provide great customer service and the sales would follow. It was a different strategy to the one I was used to, which was about sales and profit first, followed by the customer and then the team.

I joined the high end coffee chain in 2001 as a District Manager. Compared to the Pizza chain this was a picnic, largely influenced by the fact that the stores were all in fairly nice areas and the opening hours were far more sociable.

After having been an Area Manager for eight years I was ready for a new challenge and moved into HR to look after resourcing for the stores. I was responsible for ensuring that we had as few management vacancies as possible. I grew the team from four to nine, taking on Head Office as well when my boss moved on, and I loved it. Then the recession of 2008/2009 hit…

Being made redundant was clearly the universe giving me a swift kick up the derriere as I absolutely feel that running my own business, using my experience to help small businesses, is what I am here to do. I have had my own business, Evolve and Grow, for seven years now, and have worked extensively with the Construction and Trades sectors. I love working with this industry because of the amount of untapped potential there is. It is literally like finding a 'plug', if you'll excuse the pun, and as soon as the hole in each business is filled, often with a system or back of house resource, the business literally takes off.

I have written this book with tradespeople in mind. Within each chapter I will share lots of practical steps which you can take and implement immediately to make a big difference in your business. I have also included case studies of clients. In addition, there are short exercises for you to complete to capture your learnings in relation to your own business.

So, let's get started!

How to use this book

I have made this book as user friendly as possible to enable you to find the information you need right now to make the biggest improvements. It is structured around the BUILD system, which is a methodology I created specifically for the Construction and Trades industries.

BUILD stands for:

- Business planning
- Understanding your strengths
- Implementing systems and processes
- Love your customer
- Develop and delegate

In Chapter 1 you will find a questionnaire to score your business in terms of its health in four distinct areas – Sales and Marketing, Customer Service, People and Finance/Systems. Depending on where your biggest challenge lies, you will then be signposted to the relevant chapter in the book to learn practical steps you can take right now to improve things.

An astounding 70% of all insolvencies in the UK are within the Construction and Trades sectors, amounting on average to around 2,500 businesses per quarter. I'm sure no-one starts a business to struggle, make little money or fail. In my experience, most tradespeople are excited by the possibilities of running their own business and are good at what they do – technically. And this is where the problem lies. They have been trained well in their profession, but at no point did their training include how to run a business, and a technically skilled tradesperson and great businessperson are two very different things.

Sadly, but perhaps not surprisingly considering the high number of Trades and Construction businesses that go under, this sector has one of the highest suicide rates. In 2016, a study conducted by the Centers for Disease Control and Prevention reported that the sector was the second highest group in the table, with 53 suicides per 100,000 people in Trades and Construction professions.

I see the stress that business owners in this sector find themselves in. They generally work hard, seldom make decent money, and are often in debt. The frustrating thing is, I frequently hear, 'I don't have the time to look at my figures, or have a meeting with my staff.' Owners are too busy working on the tools, heads down, and this is one of the key problems.

The seven main challenges

These are the seven main challenges I find in Construction and Trades businesses:

- Lack of organisation
- Lack of systems and process
- Lack of visibility of meaningful financial information which then limits decision making
- Lack of resource in the right place, effectively capping the growth of the business
- Lack of working capital
- Poor cash flow
- Low profit margins.

In this book, I will take you step by step through how to overcome each of these challenges, essentially the basics in how to run a business – something that probably wasn't covered when you learnt your trade. I was lucky enough to learn these practices while working for large established organisations, and have taken them into the world of small business with considerable success. None of it is rocket science; in fact, in my experience it is often the simple things that work the best.

Here are some common statements I hear:

I can't afford to take anyone on to do X, Y and Z. I often find it is the opposite: you can't afford *not* to take someone on. Not having someone looking after invoicing, the booking of jobs and chasing of payments can have a huge impact on cash flow and customer experience. This is why it is so important to have a close handle on the figures, e.g. assistance with admin and bookkeeping, to predict what is likely to come in and see the impact on profit of a small investment.

It's all in my head. I have never worked with any other type of client with such an ability to remember all the jobs they have on – who needs to be invoiced, materials that need to be ordered, etc., etc. That's great, but I can't imagine that you can remember everything, not to mention the amount of stress that this causes, zapping your energy.

I don't have the time to... This is the problem with not having a plan and a structured working week in place. Without having time set aside to manage the business, you are likely to be fire-fighting – responding to whatever you feel is the most urgent demand on your time.

I'm fed up with people not doing what they are meant to. Finding, developing and retaining good people is a common challenge in any business, but especially so in the Trades and Construction industries. Poorly performing people can cost time and money, not to mention stress. Recruitment is not an exact science, but with a process in place it is possible to increase the likelihood of finding and identifying good people, and then developing and keeping them.

I have no idea how much money I am turning over or how much profit I am making. If there is only one thing you take away from this book, please let it be *you have to know your numbers.* Unless you know how much you are making from each job and your future cash flow, it is impossible to make informed decisions. What then happens is often procrastination, i.e. you never make a decision, and the task of finding someone to help is always tomorrow's task.

This book won't teach you how to fix a leaking tap, or re-wire a house, or build a conservatory. Trust me, you wouldn't want my help with those things. But what I do know well is how to run a business, and I have helped several business owners in the Trades and Construction field make the jump from working on the tools to working on the business, driving sales and profit. And I love it! There is no better feeling than helping people succeed financially and personally, seeing the positive effects this has on their health, family, relationships…need I go on?

My practical strategies will help you create the business you have always dreamed of having, giving you back time and money and taking away stress.

Sounds good? Then read on.

The BUILD System

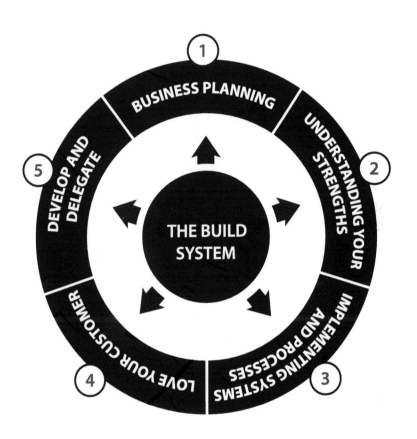

Chapter 1

BUSINESS PLANNING

In this chapter, I will take you through the most common problems I see tradespeople incur through a lack of proper business planning. The tips and techniques I share are all easy to implement and only require you to sit somewhere you won't be disturbed so that you can step out of your business and put some plans in place.

To be successful, all you need to do is keep the four basic elements of any business in balance. By completing a short questionnaire, you will be able to highlight where they are out of balance in your business and where the opportunity lies.

Some questions to ask yourself if you have a Construction or Trades business are:

- How well do you know your numbers?
- How good would you say your cash flow is?

How much working capital (cash in bank) do you have to cover the business in the event of an emergency?

There are simple processes to address all of these issues. By implementing just one of them, you will see a difference to the financial health of your business.

If you don't know where you are going,
any road will get you there.
Lewis Carroll

It's true. Unless you take some time out of your business to plan, think about what you would like to be different and where you would like to be a year from now, then it is pot luck whether or not you will end up there.

Future vision

A powerful exercise I learnt from one of my mentors, Roger James Hamilton http://www.rogerjameshamilton.com/, Founder of Entrepreneurs Institute http://entrepreneursinstitute.com and the creator of GeniusU, Wealth Dynamics and Talent Dynamics, is called 'Future Vision'. This is a process of imagining that you are fast forwarding 12 months and everything is different. Things have transformed and everything is as you wish.

If everything was as you wished it would be in your business, what would be different? Would it be more sales, more profit? How much? How would you feel? Better organised? Less stressed? Take a moment to make a list and include specifics wherever possible.

Goals and purpose

There is a need for setting both short- and long-term goals. Always start with the long-term goals. It is far easier to think about the long-term future as we then forget about the challenges we are facing today.

Here are some key differences to think about. Apply the following questions to the long-term (three years) first. Then work your way back from three years and set smaller goals, asking the same questions in relation to the medium-term (two years) and finally the short-term (one year):

- What would you like to be turning over?
- How many people would you need as employees and/or subcontractors?
- How many vans would you need on the road?
- How much profit would you like to make?
- What support staff would you need, e.g. office assistant, financial controller?
- Would you need an office, or a bigger office?

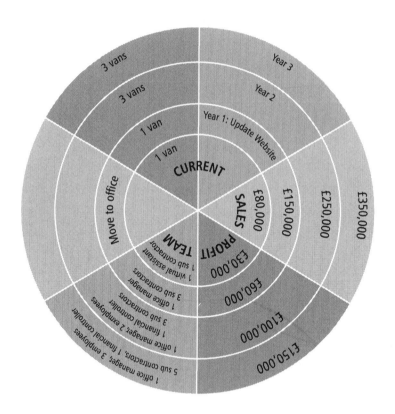

By the time you get to the short-term goals, it should be easier to set them without today's challenges getting in the way.

Unless you have a clear purpose, a reason to get out of bed every morning, it will be very difficult to motivate yourself, especially when you inevitably hit challenging times.

Your purpose may be nothing to do with what the business does. It may be what financial success enables you to do, e.g. giving your children certain opportunities. Alternatively, it may be that you care deeply about the service your business provides, and your clear purpose is to offer an exceptional level of care to your customers. If this is not something you have thought about particularly, I would strongly recommend you take some time out to do so. Having a clear purpose and goals can give you something to aim for, rather than just going through the day-to-day monotony.

Understanding the numbers

Once you have an idea of what you would like to be different, in order to make any changes, it is important you have a strong handle on the figures. It is difficult to make any meaningful decisions that involve additional costs without seeing exactly where you are. Getting up to date meaningful financial information on a business in this industry is itself often a challenge, but you need to do it, even if it is your most recent year-end accounts, which I am aware may look like gobbledygook. Don't worry, I will walk you through exactly where to look.

Here is an example of a company's year-end accounts explained in plain English.

PIPE DREAM PLUMBERS LTD

Detailed Profit and Loss Account for the Year Ended 31 December 2016

	2016	2015	Notes
			The two columns relate to the most recent year and the year prior
	£	£	
Turnover	£289,653	£217,635	This is the total amount of net sales over the year (without VAT)
Cost of Sales			
Purchases	£97,613	£76,172	These are the materials bought
Sub Contractor Labour	£23,172	£39,174	These are the costs of sub contractors i.e. any plumber who is not on the payroll
Total	£120,785	£115,346	Purchases + Sub Contractors
Gross Profit	£168,868	£102,289	This is the amount of profit left when sub contractor costs and purchases are deducted from sales
Semi-Variable costs			Otherwise referred to as overheads – what the business has spent over the year in the various areas
Advertising and marketing	£3,373	£2,435	e.g. website, advertising, marketing
Audit and Accountancy	£1,084	£1,167	
Bad Debt	£673	£465	unpaid invoices
Bank Fees	£266	£358	bank charges
Directors Renumeration	£11,000	£11,000	basic salary of director, all other income is taken from profit as dividends generally
Entertainment	£633	£456	
General Expenses	£716	£1,235	costs that can't be attributed to one of the cost lines
Insurance	£2,878	£2,567	
IT software and maintenance	£1,543	£867	computer costs
Motor Vehicle expenses	£5,341	£4,356	fuel, maintenance on vans
Pension	£1,200	£1,200	
Printing and Stationary	£276	£356	
Staff training	£1,119	£878	

Notes

Subscriptions	£615	£567	any memberships
Telephone and Internet	£1,549	£1,456	
Travel	£572	£875	
Wages and Salaries	£72,413	£43,527	costs of employees on the payroll
Total semi-variable costs	£105,251	£73,765	all the semi-variable costs added together
Net Profit	£63,617	£28,524	This the profit made before tax is paid i.e. Net sales – Purchases – Sub Contractors – Semi-variable costs

Enter your company's year-end figures in a table similar to the one below. You can download a free table from www.evolveandgrowcoaching.com/book-downloads...

		£	% of sales
A	Sales		
B	Materials		e.g. material costs divided by sales costs x 100
C	Subcontractor labour		
D	Gross profit (A minus B minus C)		
E	Overheads		
F	Operating profit (D minus E)		

Cost of sales. Put simply, these are the costs incurred if you make a sale, e.g. materials and subcontractor labour. You will only spend something on these areas if you actually make a sale.

Gross profit. Our sales minus the cost of sales leaves us with gross profit. The percentage of sales that this is can vary from one trade to the other.

Overheads. Also referred to as semi-variable costs, these are the costs that you have in running the business regardless of whether or not you make a sale, e.g. rent, salaries, insurance, etc. Some of these will remain static, e.g. rent. Others may increase as sales increase, e.g. you may need to employ more people, hence salaries would increase.

Operating profit. Also referred to as 'net profit before income tax' or 'earnings before income tax, depreciation and amortisation (EBITDA)', this is the amount of profit you have made, on which you have to pay 20% corporation tax (at present) if you are a Limited company. This is another reason why it is important to know your numbers, so that you can ensure you are putting sufficient aside for tax. Good practice is to put 20% of operating profit into a separate tax account.

Generally in this industry there is no shortage of demand for one's service, i.e. most business owners know that if they had more people, or were better organised and took every call and followed up on every quote, they would easily increase their sales. If this is the case for you, enter what you think your sales could be in the table similar to the one below. You can download a free table on www.evolveandgrowcoaching.com/book-downloads

		£	% of sales
A	Sales		
B	Materials	% from above x forecasted sales, e.g. 30% would be 0.3 x sales	
C	Subcontractor labour	Repeat as above	
D	Gross profit (A minus B minus C)		
E	Overheads		
F	Operating profit (D minus E)		

We now need to know how many additional jobs this increase in sales equates to, and for this we need to know the average value of each job. This will be an estimate, and the easiest way to do this is to estimate how many jobs you completed each week for the financial year, relating to the year-end accounts you have in front of you.

For example:

Annual sales	£147,895
Approximate number of weekly customers = 10	10 x 52 Weeks = 520 customers
Average value of client	£147,895 divided by 520 = £284

In this example, if we want to increase the sales to £200,000, we will need to service an additional 183 customers a year (3.5 a week). £200,000 – £147,895 = £52,105; £52,105 divided by average value of customer (£284) = 183; 183 divided by 52 weeks = 3.5.

The reason why we represent certain costs as a percentage of sales is that as sales increase, the percentage of these costs will remain the same. E.g. if materials are 30% of sales, this is likely to remain the same regardless of the volume of sales. This is also likely to be true with the percentage of subcontractor labour. However, overheads won't remain the same percentage of sales as the volume increases. A cost such as telephone or broadband is a constant, unless you install additional phone lines. You may, though, choose to acquire an additional van or take someone else on to the payroll which would increase the cost of these lines.

Make a note of what extra resources you would need, to deal with the amount of target sales that you have written down, e.g. extra van, an office assistant, etc. Now write down the approximate extra cost that this would incur and include it in the overheads box.

We now have a financial forecast in place. We know:

- What sales we want to achieve
- How much we would be spending on the different lines
- How much operating profit we would make

This is effectively our map that we will check in against each month to see if what we predicted is happening.

Pricing a job

In my experience, this is a common area where business owners come unstuck. Often quotes are done on 'the back of a fag packet', i.e. quickly scribbled down, calculating the cost of materials, labour and then an amount added on for profit. The problem is that this is often not accurate, and because of the fear of not winning the work, the business owner tries to quote as cheap a price as possible. To top it all, they often don't have the correct systems in place to show afterwards if any profit has been made on the job, and therefore the cycle continues.

A CRM system such as Tradify www.tradifyhq.com or simPRO www.simpro.co.uk (referred to in more detail in Chapter 3) can assist with the quoting process. There is also specific software for producing accurate quotes such as https://www.estimate.co.uk.

CASE STUDY
The importance of understanding the numbers

Often, I find that a tradesperson's strength lies with people, i.e. seeing potential clients and winning business. In many cases, it isn't in back of house activities such as tracking and analysing the financial performance of the business. And even when it is, the owner usually hasn't been developed to make the most of their strengths.

This was the case with Lee, the owner of a garage who was referred to me by a mutual colleague. When Lee arrived for his consultation, I could immediately tell that he was bright. However, he was extremely stressed with his business, and had a belief that it couldn't be any other way. He had almost resigned himself to the fact that it was impossible to make money in an ethical way in the garage industry.

What also struck me was his strong commitment to the customer, his values around charging a fair price. He honestly thought it was impossible to charge a price that was fair to the customer and produce sufficient profit for the business.

We began working together the following month, and the first thing we did, like I do with all clients, was to get under the skin of the numbers. I profiled him (more of this in Chapter 2), and discovered that he had a natural propensity for numbers; he just needed some training to make the most of it.

Unfortunately, it wasn't that simple. I also discovered that materials (cost of sales) were running at 60% of sales – no wonder he was stressed! This left only 40% for overheads – rent, salaries, heating, lighting, marketing, etc. This simply wasn't enough to make any profit.

When I dug a bit deeper, I discovered that not only was the pricing structured in a way that made the margins too small, but the business wasn't charging for collecting and dropping off vehicles. Some of Lee's customers lived a considerable distance from the garage and this was costing him heavily in terms of fuel and labour.

Energised by detail and the numbers, Lee took to what we did next like a duck to water. We implemented an accounting software solution called Xero (more about this in Chapter 3). I taught him how to create a financial forecast, how to input this into Xero and run reports, and crucially how to calculate the price he needed to be charging on each job.

By making sure that the cost of the parts was always 50% of sales or less, Lee ensured that there was always enough profit to pay for the running costs of the business and leave a small amount. He also created a system that calculated a fair price to charge for collection and delivery depending on the distance the customer lived from the garage.

These small changes – forecasting, accounting software, and a method to ensure the right price was charged – really changed things. My concern, as it always is when I begin working with a client, was whether Lee was going to be able to make the mindset change required. The first few weeks are crucial, because they are about taking some steps that undoubtedly will feel uncomfortable. Remember, Lee was of the belief that it was impossible to have happy customers who were charged a fair price and make a profit.

Six months down the line, Lee had grown sales by 24%, given himself and his business partner a salary increase and made a profit of 7%, compared to breaking even the previous year. This alone would have been rewarding, but what was even more so was seeing Lee's change in demeanour and mindset. He was dreaming of what else was possible, not just with his business, but also in other areas of his life.

It is at times like these that I feel very lucky to be able to do what I do.

KPIs and Critical Indicators

There is a big difference between what we call Key Performance Indicators (KPIs) and Critical Indicators. KPIs are what appear on the Profit and Loss account, e.g. the figures that represent what has been and gone – it is a bit like looking in the rear view mirror of our business. It is important to review these, of course, but there isn't anything we can do to change them.

Critical Indicators are metrics that need to be tracked on a daily and weekly basis. Every business will have between three and five of them. Think of them like a set of traffic lights that alert you to a potential problem, giving you time to react and take action before it is too late.

In the Trades and Construction industries, examples of Critical Indicators are:

- Number of new enquiries
- Number of quotes submitted
- Number of quotes resulting in business

- Percentage of jobs on track to timeline set
- Labour hours used v forecast

If one of these began to go in the wrong direction and you were tracking it weekly, you would be able to react and take action (hopefully) in time.

Profit and loss, balance sheet and cash flow

I am often asked by clients, 'So if that is how much profit I am making, how come it's not in my bank account?' The trouble is that few accountants, in my experience, take the time to explain to their clients the difference between the three key financial reports in any business. I probably should thank them as this contributes towards me being so busy!

In laymen's terms, here is the difference between the three reports:

Profit and loss. A profit and loss account simply shows how much you have invoiced, how much you have spent on the sale (e.g. materials and subcontractor labour), how much you are spending on running the business (overheads) and how much profit you have made altogether on jobs. There are some key reasons why the profit is not showing in your bank account:

- Cash flow, i.e. the customers have not yet paid their invoices
- You are financing the jobs, i.e. you are buying the materials, but there is a time lag before the customer pays you

- You are paying for materials on a credit card and this is not being submitted to the accounting software system
- You are taking too much money out of the business

Balance sheet. The balance sheet shows the business's assets (those which it owns) together with debtors (people who owe it money) and cash reserves, as well as liabilities/creditors to whom it owes money, e.g. outstanding supplier invoices.

Cash flow statement. This shows the expected receipts of cash based on what has been sold and when payments are expected. It will also show what is due to be leaving the business, e.g. in the form of payments to suppliers.

CASE STUDY
The importance of analysing the numbers

I was referred to a local glazing company by its accountant a few years ago. The business owner, George, was clearly a 'people' person – he enjoyed being out there, doing the work, but also knew that for the business to grow and for him to be less stressed, he desperately needed systems and processes.

I discovered that there wasn't any analysis of the figures taking place. George had Sage, another accounting software package, in place, but wasn't running any reports to analyse the figures. Hence he wasn't identifying critical factors, such as the amount that was owing to the business in terms of unpaid invoices, some going back several months, if not years.

Shortly after we started working together, George hired an Operations Manager, Mark – without my help, I might add! Mark had experience in the industry, and George was desperate. Panic hiring is something that I often see, and we'll cover it more in Chapter 5.

By this point, we had monthly profit and loss reports running, and George and I were sitting down to review them each month. We were therefore able to spot pretty soon that material costs were rising as a percentage of sales at an alarming rate. Upon further investigation, we discovered that although Mark had experience in the glazing industry, he was making crucial mistakes left, right and centre. If measurements are just 1–2 mm out, the glass cannot be used, causing costly wastage to the business. Fortunately, George was able to spot this fairly soon and take action, but had he not been analysing the figures, it would have gone undetected for a lot longer.

Working capital

Do you have enough working capital? This is the amount of money you have in the bank to give you breathing space, e.g. should you need to finance a job by ordering the parts before receiving the money. Generally speaking, this figure should be three times your overheads. So if it costs £6,000 a month to operate your business, ideally you should always have £18,000 or more in the bank.

I recently met with a construction firm which specialised in building high-end market homes, all in the £2–5 million bracket. It amazed me how close to the wind it was operating. There were few reserves in the bank account, which meant that it would only take one customer not to pay an instalment on the project and the business would potentially go under. This is one reason why there are so many insolvencies in this sector – yes, it is often due to lack of organisation and financial analysis, but sometimes it is due to the fact that business owners are just taking on too much risk.

Tony Hawkes of Asset Finance Solutions http://www.asset financesolutions.com/ offers asset finance to businesses to help them have the important buffer of working capital in place. Here is what he has to say:

In the Trades industries, business owners often think, I can do this for myself, and become a victim of their own success. They don't appreciate that in order to go to the next level, they need more capital in the business. The issue is to actually obtain that kind of funding. The banks don't seem willing to lend because their criteria has changed from what it used to be, and therefore business owners panic when they are in a hole rather than planning and getting ahead of the game. Once you get ahead of the game, you are laughing. You can then take it to the next level.

Understanding what the funding gap is, is also important. Ideally you want your customers to pay you quicker than you pay your suppliers. Often what might happen is a supplier reduces their payment terms from 90 to 60 days, for example, but the speed at which customers are paying their bills does not change. This can have a massive impact on cash flow.

Managing cash flow

Do you have a process in place to manage cash flow? It doesn't matter how many sales you are making, until the money is in your bank account, you run the risk of being a busy fool.

The general pattern I see is business owners rushing around seeing customers, checking on jobs and running off to get materials that haven't been ordered. They then get home in the evening and set about preparing quotes to email to customers, and this often spills over into the weekend. They are often simply too tired to get around to doing the invoices, so this takes a back seat, getting done too far down the line. Hence it is often the business financing the job – if you need to order £2,000 worth of materials for a job, but you are not invoicing the customer until six weeks later, this is six weeks that you are carrying this cost.

Cash is king! We need it in the bank account as soon as possible, and want to be carrying as little risk as possible to ensure we stay financially healthy. I'm sure the majority of insolvencies are not due to a lack of customers, but rather poor cash flow, poor profit margins and taking on too much risk.

As I will advise frequently, find someone who can manage the whole back of house operation efficiently. Don't try and do it yourself. Often it won't be your strength, and this employee will more than pay for themselves (see Chapter 2). By using accounting software such as Xero, your office assistant can create invoices quickly and send them to the customer, along with automatic reminders if the bill is not paid.

How do you know which jobs are profitable? By having accounting software in place (see Chapter 3), it is possible to set up each job with a different cost centre. Providing costs for those particular jobs is attributed to the relevant cost centre. It is then possible to report on the profitability of each job, which is a must in the Trades and Construction industries. But it is often one of the key processes that I find missing in Trade businesses.

Terms and conditions

Having clear terms and conditions of business in place ensures that you are less likely to have problems with non-payment of invoices further down the line. It also sets you apart from the competition that hasn't bothered and places you in the 'professional' camp.

The other important reason to have terms and conditions in place is so that if you are unfortunate enough not to have received a customer's payment after three reminders, you have the option to take them to a small claims court. If you don't have any terms and conditions in place, it can make it less likely that you will be successful in your claim.

These are not prescriptive, but as a general guideline, it is a good idea to send an email when the invoice becomes 7, 14 and 21 days overdue, supported by a phone call to the debtor. The emails can be automated using a system such as Xero and the phone calls outsourced to a bookkeeper or virtual assistant if you don't have an office assistant in place. I cannot stress enough that the reminders should never be sent by you, for two reasons – 1) you'll instantly appear to be a one-man band and lose credibility, and 2) it can have a negative effect on your relationship with the customer.

If you have followed all your internal processes correctly – the quote was sent out with terms and conditions; the invoice was sent out on time; reminders were emailed and supported with a phone call – and your customer still has yet to pay, what is the best way to manage this?

My recommendation would be to hand it over to a reputable debt collection agency. Yes, the debt collectors will take a percentage of the bill if they're successful in retrieving payment, but trust me, it is well worth it. They are the experts in getting customers to pay, and again show that you are serious about collecting the money. They will also advise you on whether or not it is worth going to a small claims court.

The four elements of a business

Any business is effectively made up of four different elements. The trick is to keep them in balance.

They are:

- Marketing
- Team
- Customer service
- Finance and systems

When I was in my resourcing role with the high-end coffee chain, my job was essentially to ensure that we had sufficient of the right people to support the substantial growth of the company. At its peak in the UK and Ireland, we were opening three new stores every week. There was obviously a considerable amount of roles to fill, in addition to natural turnover of positions. Customer service could have been at risk because of the changes made within teams, so we had to be very careful in managing this expansion.

Here are some case studies of businesses I have worked with illustrating typical scenarios:

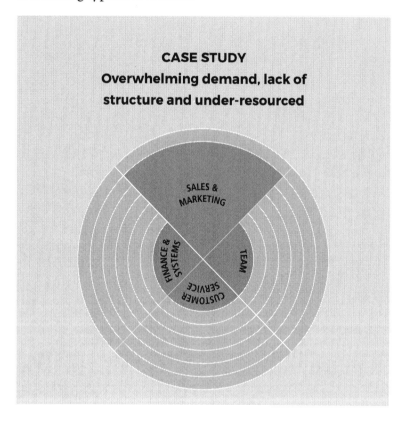

CASE STUDY
Overwhelming demand, lack of structure and under-resourced

This construction business had no shortage of demand, but there was no structure in place to deal with it. The business owner was trying to do everything himself. Even though he actually had all the people he needed to support him, he hadn't defined what their roles should be and struggled to let go. Customer service was massively impacted due to the fact that he wasn't getting back to customers with a quote following the initial visit. This led to a vicious circle (see diagram below).

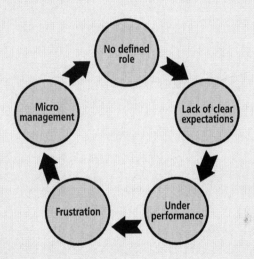

The irony was that all he needed to do was identify who should be doing what according to their strengths and let go. As soon as he did this, it was like finding and fixing the leak in his business, which was then allowed to flow.

CASE STUDY
Over investment

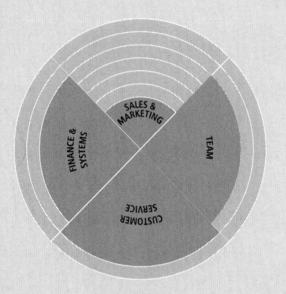

In this scenario, the client had invested heavily in having the right systems and processes in place. He was providing great customer service, and had good relationships with quality people for when he needed to outsource. The problem was that he had no marketing plan in place, which over time could have taken the business under due to over investment – investing too much ahead of the curve.

CASE STUDY
Further growth stunted by lack of
people systems and processes

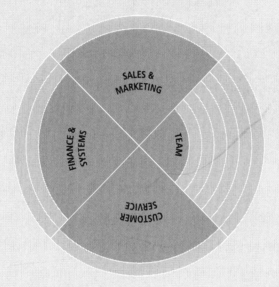

In this business, my client was providing excellent customer service – we knew this because he was measuring it. His company had also gone through significant organic growth; all his new business came through client referrals.

When he initially came to see me, he intuitively knew that the business was at risk and wouldn't be able to grow unless he had help to put some structures in place around people. This involved putting in various systems and processes to help him measure, manage and reward performance as well as those to help him identify and recruit the right talent.

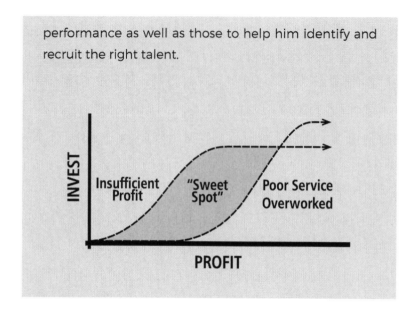

What I often see in Trades

Invariably what I see within Trades businesses in regards to the four elements is that sales and marketing is not an issue. Often the business owners I have worked with are very good at their trade, so they start a business, providing a good service. Customers then recommend them and the business grows, sometimes at an alarming rate.

The owners take people on, often friends or family, which can be a problem in itself, and before they know it, they are running a business as opposed to just selling their time for money. The problem is they are still doing this as well, they are still on the tools, so all the important tasks such as invoicing, chasing payments, managing people, etc. take a back seat.

The result? A lot of stress for the business owner, and often a poor customer experience and poor cash flow. Most businesses, especially in this industry, do not go under due to lack of demand for the service. Far from it. It is for other reasons, such as the speed at which invoices go out, debtors often not being chased for payment of invoices in a timely manner, and customer service not being measured.

Let me explain a little more about the four elements.

Marketing

Product/service. Are you providing what the market wants? What makes your offering unique? I often hear people describe their unique selling proposition (USP) as 'great customer service' or 'a family business that really cares'. I'm sorry, but this doesn't cut it. Most businesses would describe themselves in this way.

What is *really* different about how you deliver your service? Have you got any feedback from your customers that verifies your claims? Surveys can be great for this. If 98% of your customers would be happy to recommend your service to friends and family, then tell people that on your website, in brochures, verbally, etc.

It is essential that you stay close to your market and are aware of any changes in its needs and wants, e.g. the advent of solar power and the impact this has had on the electrical and plumbing industries. Remain relevant.

The world is moving at an alarming rate and it is easy to lose sight of this. Just look at what happened to the likes of HMV, Blockbuster and some high street travel agents. They saw the change too late, or failed to adapt in time.

Effectiveness of your marketing strategy, i.e. the channels you use to get new customers, e.g. a website, networking, social media, trade websites, etc. Do you know where your business comes from? How effective is it vs how much you are spending in terms of time and money on that channel? How much does it cost to get a new lead?

Customer service

Are you measuring the service your company provides? So often I ask clients, 'Do you think you provide good customer service?' and invariably the answer is yes. However, when we either have a mystery shop conducted or undertake a customer survey, the story can be quite different.

It is important that you ask your customers if they are happy with the service you provide. Often if companies do this at all, they do it in person. Nothing wrong with that necessarily, and if this is you, you are in the minority in a good way. However, in the UK especially, people are very good at saying everything is fine when it isn't. They then moan to everyone but the person who should be hearing it.

There are several benefits to conducting surveys or regular mystery shops. I cover this more in Chapter 4.

Have you conducted any market research? This can be an invaluable exercise for two main reasons:

Benchmarking of pricing. See where your pricing falls in relation to the market. One client I worked with was able to increase his turnover by 10% just by increasing his prices. The benchmarking exercise (calling competitors) gave him confidence as he could see he was one of the cheapest garages in the area, and more often than not providing better service than his competitors.

Staying close to changing market trends. OK, the Trades and Construction industries perhaps don't change as much or as quickly as some, but all industries are constantly evolving. Often, I ask clients to think of well-known companies which have failed, and the reason can usually be linked back to them not responding quickly enough to changing market trends.

Team

Do you have sufficient people? Sometimes it is obvious that a business hasn't got enough people, and this in itself is preventing business growth. In some cases, it is having a detrimental impact on customer service. Other times, it's just that people are not in the right roles or not being utilised effectively.

Are they capable? Do you have the right people for the job itself? Have they been trained sufficiently? Do they know what is expected of them?

Don't immediately write people off who are not performing. Often they can be turned around with a back to basics conversation and re-setting expectations. I cover this in far more detail in Chapter 6.

Are they engaged? When people are engaged, they stay, strive and thrive. In other words, they don't leave, they work hard to do better and they grow in capability. It is not about just being satisfied; engagement is one step up. When you have an engaged team, everything is so much easier. They think for themselves, go out of their way to do more than what is expected, and ultimately free you up to run the business.

Finance and systems

Is the business reaching its sales targets, and is it profitable? Invariably people are not able to answer these questions when they don't have the right systems in place to make this information visible. Sometimes they don't even know the turnover of the business, let alone how much money they are making. As mentioned before, this makes it very difficult for them to make informed decisions.

Is cash flow a problem? Often the business doesn't have a sales problem, it has a cash flow problem due to a delay in invoices being sent out and debtors not being chased.

Are you utilising IT systems? Accounting software such as Xero or Sage, if set up correctly, can provide useful reports that help you make better decisions. In the Trade and Construction industries, it is also important to have the system set up to report on individual job profitability.

A customer relationship management (CRM) system specifically for Trades, e.g. simPRO, Powered Now or Tradify, can help your business schedule labour and jobs as well as send marketing to your customers.

Exercise

MARKETING	Yes/No
Channels	
Are you attracting enough new customers?	
Do you have an up to date website?	
Have you tried networking?	
Do you have relationships with key professions who can pass you business, and whom you can help in return?	
Product	
Are there any products or services that your customers want that you could be offering?	
Key question – are you getting sufficient leads and enquiries?	

CUSTOMER SERVICE	Yes/No
Experience	
Do you measure the customer service you are providing?	
Are there bottlenecks in the business?	

Market research	
Do you know what the latest trends are in your field and what the market is wanting?	
Are you charging enough?	
Key question – do customers readily refer and recommend you?	

TEAM	Yes/No
Numbers	
Do you have enough people?	
Ability	
Are they doing their job to standard?	
Attitude	
Are they keen to come to work and do a good job?	
Do they take feedback well?	
Are they reliable?	
Key question – are you happy with your team?	

FINANCE AND SYSTEMS	Yes/No
Sales and profit	
Do you have a financial forecast in place?	
Is your business growing?	
Is it profitable?	
Do you know this for certain?	
Cash flow	
Are invoices being sent out promptly?	
Is there a process in place to chase non-payments and deal with debtors?	
Systems	
Is there accounting software in place providing financial visibility?	
Is there a customer relationship management system in place specific to the Trade industry?	
Are your processes sufficiently documented, enabling others to be trained?	
Key question – do you feel you have the right systems and processes in place to provide you with information and create organisation?	

You should now have visibility of which element of your business needs attention first to bring it into balance. In my experience of working with Trades, marketing is rarely the issue. Businesses in this industry have plenty of demand for their services. The problem is often that they have no visibility of their finances, which is having a negative impact on their ability to make good decisions.

Below are some simple steps to take, depending on where you have the most 'no' answers. More detail on each step is provided later in the book, so you may decide to use this exercise as a signpost then head straight to the relevant chapter.

Finance and systems are my opportunity:

- I need accounting software (Chapter 3)
- I need a customer relationship management (CRM) system (Chapter 3)
- I need to complete a full financial forecast (Chapter 1)
- I need cash flow management processes (Chapter 1)

People are my opportunity:

- I need to establish what roles and responsibilities are needed in my team (Chapter 2)
- I need to find and recruit the right people (Chapter 5)
- I need to improve the performance of my team (Chapter 6)

Customer service is my opportunity:

- I need to begin measuring the experience that my customers have (Chapter 4)
- I need to establish where it is going wrong (Chapter 4)
- I need to identify where there are bottlenecks (Chapter 4)

Marketing is my opportunity:

- I need to identify how to make networking work (Chapter 7)
- I would like to form effective partnerships with other trades (Chapter 7)

Now you have an understanding of the four key elements of any business and where the opportunities within your business lie, along with an appreciation of how important it is to have a close understanding of your numbers. Although it doesn't have to be you doing all of this, you can delegate, but you can't abdicate.

Remember to set your destination (goals), create the map (financial forecast) and check in regularly to make sure you are on track.

Chapter 2

UNDERSTANDING YOUR STRENGTHS

In this chapter we look at how to identify and make better use of your strengths. These are the skills and qualities that you have; the things that come most naturally to you. When you play to your strengths, you are completely energised and you add the most value.

We are brought up in a world where we are encouraged to try and be a 'good all-rounder', but there is no such thing. I know this is a generalisation, but in my experience business owners in the Construction and Trades industries often didn't enjoy or do that well at school. They are very practical people; it's just that their strengths were not developed within the traditional educational environment.

I frequently meet people who were, directly or indirectly, told they 'wouldn't make anything of themselves', they were 'naughty and disruptive', and maybe even not that bright. It is very sad, but it is also why I love working with these industries, developing untapped potential and helping people achieve far more than they perhaps thought was possible.

The concept of 'flow'

The concept of 'flow' was developed by a Hungarian psychologist Mihaly Csikszentmihalyi. When we are in 'flow', we are loving what we are doing, the time flies and we are operating at our best. Every time I describe this state to clients and ask them to tell me about a time when they were in flow, we find that it wasn't necessarily while they were doing an easy task. There is always a certain amount of challenge when we're in flow, but it is an enjoyable challenge.

If we find something too challenging, we can move into anxiety and ultimately stress. Conversely, if we are doing something that we don't enjoy but find easy, we move into complacency and boredom. This is why it is key to understand our teams, so we can ensure that they are challenged by what they are doing and enjoy the job. Otherwise it will always be difficult to have a high performing team. Check out Chapter 5 which takes you through how to identify this at the recruitment stage to ensure that you hire the right people.

Playing to our strengths

I first came across the concept of focusing on developing strengths as opposed to weaknesses seven years ago when I met James Brook and Dr Paul Brewerton, who co-founded Strengths Partnership Ltd in the UK. They created an assessment tool called Strengthscope® which I began using with clients when I first started the business. It is a test that you complete online which highlights your seven key strengths out of a possible 24.

You can read more about Strengthscope® here https://www. strengthscope.com/

Many people are completely unaware of their strengths, possibly because we live in a society that focuses on weaknesses and eradicating them. With Strengthscope®, we don't ignore weaknesses, but we approach them in a different way. More of this later, but first and foremost we must focus on developing our strengths and learn about the potential flip side of them.

When we overuse our strengths, we call that a strength going into overdrive. Our strengths are the things that naturally energise us, and because of this we can sometimes use them too much.

I often cite the examples of famous people like Lady Margaret Thatcher to demonstrate. Lady Thatcher, I would guess, had strengths of self-confidence and decisiveness, coupled with potentially low empathy. When self-confidence goes into overdrive, we can appear arrogant and dismissive of feedback from those around us. Equally when decisiveness is in overdrive, we can make decisions too quickly to our detriment. In the case of Lady Thatcher, many of those around her were trying to provide advice, but it fell on deaf ears. She ploughed ahead anyway, and of course the rest is history. Her team turned against her and she resigned.

The following table shows all 24 strengths, their descriptions if the strength is being used well, and what happens if the strength goes into overdrive. Interestingly, we frequently find that it is our strengths that can cause more of a problem than our weaknesses by being overused:

Relational – people focused		
Strength	**If being used well**	**Watch out for the overdrive**
Collaboration	You co-operate with others to overcome conflict and work towards a common goal	You may look to others to get their agreement which slows down your decision making
Compassion	You care about others, are kind and a good listener	People may take advantage of you and your caring nature
Developing others	You enjoy helping people develop, you see their strengths and their potential	You may spend too much time helping someone improve at the expense of something else
Empathy	You find it easy to step into someone else's shoes and see things from their point of view	You could lose the ability to see things objectively, agreeing with the other person too readily

Leading	You enjoy leading a team, motivating and inspiring them	You may slip into micro-managing people when it isn't needed
Persuasiveness	You enjoy debating, bringing people round to your way of thinking	You could debate for debate's sake, regardless of the usefulness of the argument
Relationship building	You are good at building networks of contacts and putting people in touch with each other	You may spend too much time doing this at the expense of something else

Execution – task focused		
Strength	**If being used well**	**Watch out for the overdrive**
Decisiveness	You find it easy to make decisions even when you may not have all the information required available	You may make decisions too quickly and then look back and either change the decision or regret it
Efficiency	You are methodical, planned and organised	You may try and fit too much in and/or be dismissive of anything that you perceive to take you off track
Flexibility	You adapt well to change and new situations	You may look for change for change's sake, and may appear restless to others
Initiative	You take action of your own accord, not waiting for others to tell you what to do	You may start too many new projects at the same time, not taking into account how likely they are to be successful

Results focused	You keep focused on the end result, and show consistent commitment throughout	In your enthusiasm to achieve results you may fail to look back to see what could be learnt or forget to recognise others
Self-improvement	You enjoy continually learning new things, developing yourself in the process	You could become a 'workshop junkie' learning lots of new things regardless of their value to the company

Thinking – task focused		
Strength	**If being used well**	**Watch out for the overdrive**
Common sense	You approach tasks in a logical manner, using your experience from previous situations	You could be dismissive of anything you consider to be a bit off the wall, preferring to stick to the tried and tested
Creativity	You enjoy coming up with innovative solutions to problems	You may come up with ideas that are not practical, overlooking the tried and tested
Critical thinking	You break things down to evaluate them, naturally spotting any risks	You could come across as being negative and/or over-critical, as you see where things could go wrong
Detail orientated	You have a strong attention to detail, regardless of the pressures	You could spend excessive time in the detail, losing sight of the big picture
Strategic minded	You enjoy looking at the big picture and are strategic in your approach	You could lose sight of the current realities as you are too focused on the big picture

Emotional – people focused		
Strength	**If being used well**	**Watch out for the overdrive**
Courage	You are prepared to take on challenges and face risks by standing up for what you believe in	You could come across as reckless or extreme when defending your beliefs and/or may take on things that are too risky
Emotional control	You are good at remaining calm and productive when under pressure	You could come across as difficult to read, not having any enthusiasm and/or aloof
Enthusiasm	You show your passion and enthusiasm openly when communicating your ideas and beliefs	You could come across as too emotional, which may discourage others from sharing their views if different
Optimism	You tend to look at the upside even during challenging times, remaining positive and believing you can influence the situation	You could fail to see areas of risk, and are unrealistically positive
Resilience	You enjoy overcoming challenges and deal well with setbacks	You could take on 'mission impossible' as you like having a challenge and winning against the odds
Self-confidence	You have a strong belief in your own abilities to get things done	You could come across as arrogant and/or be dismissive of feedback

CASE STUDY
Developing awareness of our strengths

I had known Mark, who had an electrical business, for a few years. He had said that there would have been little point in working with me previously, as there wasn't anything that needed to be done. However, now he felt like he had 'an avalanche' of business.

Great, I thought, *and I get to push the snow up the hill.*

Putting him through Strengthscope®, I identified that he had a 'leading' strength that was potentially being under-utilised. He was naturally good with people and his team was loyal to him, but he had never had any training in how to get the best from them.

Mark's leading strength was in danger at times of going into overdrive, and this showed itself as him visiting sites and taking over. If he found one of his team doing something incorrectly, he had a tendency to finish the job himself, which of course was fairly demoralising for his team.

Once he had identified this, he was more self-aware and therefore more able to adapt his approach to a coaching style rather than telling.

The result? His team grew in confidence and began making decisions of their own accord, which in turn freed Mark up to focus on more strategic activities that drove the business forward as he could trust his team.

The importance of balance in a team

An assessment that I always use with clients is Wealth Dynamics. This was developed by my mentor Roger James Hamilton http://www.rogerjameshamilton.com/ and is used by over 700,000 entrepreneurs around the world. It is based on the principles of focusing on what comes most naturally to you and surrounding yourself with others who love doing the things you hate.

If there is anything you take from this book, let this be one of the key points. I have seen businesses grow rapidly by embracing this concept, rather than the owner trying to be good at everything. If it is being out and about seeing clients that you enjoy, then do this. If it is being in the background putting systems and processes in place, then do this, but don't try and do both.

This assessment highlights which of eight profiles is your natural role, and the seat in which you should sit within your business. In summary, we have four key energies:

Dynamo – these people are very creative, and are good at coming up with new ideas. They are intuitive and are great at looking at a long-term vision of how the company could grow.

Blaze – often the primary energy for tradespeople. These individuals love being out and about seeing clients and the team, and are often naturally good at sales, enjoying activities such as networking.

Tempo – these people are service orientated and are the opposite of the Dynamo energy. They can naturally sense if clients or the team are happy and what to do to adjust if they're not. They also have a natural sense of timing.

Steel – this is all about the detail, so these people enjoy analysing the numbers and looking at trends. They are often good at thinking in a logical manner and can plan out projects really well.

Understanding the primary strengths of yourself and your team is key as it identifies what potentially is missing. Basically, you need a mix of the different energies in the business for it to be balanced. This does not necessarily mean that you have to employ lots of people. It can be just as effective to bring someone into the team in an outsourced capacity, e.g. to do bookkeeping. I personally don't have any employees in my team. Emma, who does my marketing, is self-employed;

Kathleen, my assistant, is too; and then I have a team of associates who work directly with the clients.

If everyone in your team is great at being out there, seeing the customers and winning the work, but there is no-one back of house ensuring that there is a process in place to deal with it, the business will fall down. This scenario may sound familiar to you, as it is the most common one that I come across when working with tradespeople.

Roles and responsibilities

Something I frequently come across is a lack of defined roles and responsibilities within Trades businesses, and this leads to the left hand not knowing what the right hand is doing.

A free test that you can ask your team to take straight away which will highlight their preference is called the Genius test. Access it here: https://www.geniusu.com/my-genius-test. This will tell you who is Dynamo, Blaze, Tempo and Steel. If you have too many people sitting in one of the quadrants, you are probably seeing the following problems in your business:

Dynamo – lots of talking about the future, people coming up with ideas, but maybe changing their minds.

Blaze – lots of talking! These people are good with people and sales come fairly naturally to them.

Tempo – these people may lack ideas to take the business forward, but will be good at planning.

Steel – these people will have a good handle on the details and possibly the numbers, but may struggle with sales.

Frequently in the Construction and Trades industries, people sit in the Dynamo and Blaze quadrants. They have lots of ideas and are good at building relationships with clients, being chatty, outgoing people. Where they often struggle is managing the back of house and ensuring that the 'machine' is operating smoothly. They usually complain about not having enough time, cash flow being an ongoing problem, and they don't feel very in control of their business.

CASE STUDY
Capping business growth by being out of balance

Jacques first came to me when his air conditioning business was in its infancy. It had turned over around £10k the previous year, and Jacques was eager to grow it. He had owned an air conditioning business before in South Africa, but it hadn't gone well for a variety of reasons.

What initially struck me about Jacques was his passion for customer service, and the speed with which he dealt with enquiries, submitted quotes and generally provided a great customer experience. Not surprisingly, this was generating quite a bit of demand in the local area as word got around that his company was good.

However, despite this, Jacques was nervous about spending money on employing people. I sensed that he had got his fingers burnt in the past.

We completed a financial forecast based on the number of enquiries he was receiving each week and the average value of each sale, and I could quickly see that there was no way on earth he could continue with his current structure. There simply was not enough resource to deal with the demand. The business was surviving on Jacques and one subcontractor who couldn't drive and was totally reliant on Jacques to ferry him around.

Jacques shared with me that his accountant wife Maggie, who had a full-time job, was doing the invoicing and quotes with him on evenings and weekends, which unsurprisingly was causing a strain and exhausting them in the process. I discovered later that cash flow was also a problem. Although the invoices were being sent out, they were often delayed and there was no process in place to chase non-payments.

After completing the financial forecast, the next thing we did was to profile Jacques using Wealth Dynamics. It turned out he was a Deal Maker – not a massive surprise to me as I could see he was fantastic at winning the work and providing great customer service. Deal Makers are a mix of the Tempo and Blaze energies, which are all about service and people respectively. What was desperately needed was the Steel energy, someone who was detailed, process minded and could bring some organisation into the business.

This is another vicious circle that I come across frequently:

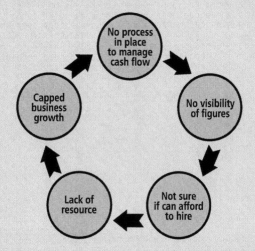

I set about explaining to Jacques the financial forecast, and the fact that he desperately needed an office assistant to process quotes, deal with enquiries, book jobs in, send invoices and chase payments. He agreed to take someone on part-time on a temporary basis, saying that he would use the person to clear the backlog and then he would be fine.

This was the November and the business was forecast to close out the year the following May on £68k. It ended up achieving £121k, and the office assistant whom we hired never left. The business went on to grow the team of subcontractors and hire another office assistant with the incumbent becoming financial controller. Eighteen months later the business had achieved just under £400k in sales.

The key points for success here are:

- Create a financial forecast which gives a clear picture of who you can afford to take on when different levels of sales have been achieved
- Understand who it is that you need and their skillset
- Invest in increasing resource sensibly, in a planned way

The eight roles in business

Within the Wealth Dynamics system there are eight defined roles that are required in any business. This doesn't mean that you need all eight; I will explain why in a moment. You can view the Wealth Dynamics square and read more about the profiles here https://www.slideshare.net/rogerjameshamilton/sample-

wealth-dynamics-report-what-entrepreneur-profile-are-you
and take the test here http://wdprofiletest.com/home/

The profiles in brief are:

Creator – these people love creating new things, find it easy
to think about the long-term vision of their company, but can
be easily distracted by what I call 'shiny new object syndrome'.

Star – these people have mainly a mix of the Dynamo and
Blaze energies, and therefore are very good at anything to do
with sales and marketing. Generating leads and public
speaking come naturally to them, but they generally don't
enjoy detail or back of house roles.

Supporter – for these people, it is all about the team and the
team's success. They therefore make natural leaders, and are
great at motivating and inspiring people. They love to talk, but
like Stars don't enjoy back of house tasks or looking at detailed
spreadsheets.

Deal maker – these people have mainly a mix of the Tempo
and Blaze energies. While they are extrovert, they tend to be
much more comfortable one on one as opposed to speaking
to a group. They are great at negotiating and closing deals, but
again are generally not good with organisation and detail.

Trader – for traders, it is all about harmony for the team and the customers. They are good at making sure everything is fair and sensing when things are not going well. They therefore make great customer service people or human resource managers. They may find thinking about the long-term vision and coming up with ideas a challenge.

Accumulator – these people enjoy detail, and because they are a mix of the Tempo and Steel energies, they are also good with timing, therefore making great project managers. They can be relied on to manage the details well and to make sure that all the elements of a project are planned out in the right order. However, don't ask them to go out networking or public speaking. They will probably hate it.

Lord – Lords tend to love numbers and the detail so they are great at finance manager roles, analysing trends and the detail behind the business. Again they are unlikely to enjoy networking and sales, preferring to be in the background where there are opportunities to drive efficiencies.

Mechanic – these people love to come in and improve the way things are done, implementing systems and processes to drive efficiencies and make things run more smoothly. They generally don't enjoy managing people or sales and marketing so much.

The 1, 2, 3 Process to forming a team

In order to ensure that your team is in balance and you aren't doing too many things yourself, here is a process that identifies the two people you need to have in the team or partner with.

Whichever profile you are, go two steps around the grid clockwise, and this profile is the first you need. You then go three steps around the grid from here, which identifies the third person.

The profiles that are on either side of our profile are what we call our secondary profiles and are also energising for us. For example, I am a Mechanic, so my secondary profiles are Lord (the numbers) and Creator (strategy, new products and services), which I also enjoy. So for each of the eight seats to be covered, follow the 1, 2, 3 Process.

Referring back to Jacques's business, I discovered he was a Deal Maker, which meant he ideally needed an Accumulator and a Creator to balance the team. We ended up hiring a Lord to manage the projects and the invoicing, while I filled the Creator seat with my secondary profile. Two years on, the business recruited an Office Manager who is a Mechanic. They have implemented enhanced systems and processes to take the business to the next level.

CASE STUDY
Growing a business by applying the Wealth Dynamics 1, 2, 3 Process

Roland joined one of my Mastermind groups in 2015. At the time his window cleaning company was predominantly just him with a couple of subcontractors. He was struggling to find the right marketing team, as the success of this type of business is based on having a volume of customers.

Roland is a Creator profile, so he needed to partner up with a Supporter (two steps around the grid) and an Accumulator (three steps further around). The Supporter would go out and make connections with additional customers, and the Accumulator would ensure that all the administration and planning happened correctly and on time.

This is exactly what Roland set about doing. He found a brilliant canvassing company which had experience in the market to go out and make additional connections, something he definitely didn't have the time to do while being busy cleaning windows.

Here is what Roland said recently to me about where he was and where his business is now:

I was struggling to find the right marketing team, i.e. canvassers...I was trying to take care of everything. [I now] have two cleaners who do the window cleaning, one admin assistant who books in the work and looks after the customers, Daniel who takes care of the marketing [the canvassing company], and in the very near future I will appoint someone in the team to look after the cleaners.

What is lovely to see is that Roland is now off the tools completely and really is the Managing Director of his own business, which has incidentally tripled its turnover in the last 18 months. He said to me, 'Wealth Dynamics shows you that you have to have people, because on your own you are physically not capable of doing everything.'

In summary, identify what activities come most naturally to you, the things that you enjoy doing the most, and surround yourself with others who love doing the things you hate. This does not mean that you can completely ignore all of those mundane tasks – the word here is delegate, not abdicate. This may feel strange as we have been brought up in an education system that has trained us to do exactly the opposite – focusing on getting better at our weaknesses. But by implementing the steps outlined in this chapter, everyone can move into flow.

And as Roger, my mentor, says, 'This is where the magic happens.'

Chapter 3

IMPLEMENTING SYSTEMS AND PROCESSES

In this chapter I will take you through proven systems and processes that work for the Construction and Trades industries. If anything, this is the most important chapter in the book, as it is these things that will ensure your business is set up for success, and you have the key information in your business visible in order to make better decisions.

I have divided the chapter into four sections: Finance, Customer, Organisational and Team.

Finance

As we covered in 'Business Planning', it is so important that you as a business owner have a strong handle on the numbers. Often I see business owners who are stressed, which is caused by them not knowing how much they are turning over each month, how much profit they are making and/or if they can afford to take someone on. The phone is ringing off the hook, but they never seem to have enough money in the bank. However, this is usually not indicative of a lack of sales. It can be a sign of not having enough time or resource to ensure invoices are sent out on time, or non-payments chased up.

Without having a clear picture of sales, profitability and cash flow, you will find it difficult to make the right decisions. This is why the first thing I ask to see when conducting a consultation with a client is their most up to date figures.

Accounting software. My personal favourite is Xero www.xero.com because it is so easy to use. It is in the cloud and it is in real time (meaning that it is always showing up to date information). It can also be accessed easily from an app on your phone, so you can check your bank balance and outstanding invoices when you are out and about. Sage is another commonly used system in the Trades industry.

Accounting software enables you to:

- Create invoices
- Produce estimates
- Track payments of suppliers
- Track payments received and reconcile against invoices
- Enter your financial forecast and report actual against it
- Produce different cost centres for each job, enabling the reporting of profitability
- Produce various reports including monthly profit and loss accounts
- Automatically send reminders for non-payment of invoices to customers when they are 7, 14 and 21 days overdue, for example

The above can save you huge amounts of time and therefore money as you can track financial information in one place. All the different software is reasonable in terms of cost as well, charging a monthly fee with no tie in to a contract.

Customer

Customer relationship management (CRM) systems enable you to have all of your customer data in one place, and market effectively to it. There are some that are specific to the Trades and Construction industries and enable you to generate quotes, schedule staff on jobs, and monitor their location.

When Construction and Trades businesses reach a certain size, it can become quite a logistical nightmare scheduling several team members on different jobs. Using a CRM system avoids mistakes being made, e.g. double booking. They are also invaluable for businesses such as a plumbing company where there may be several plumbers out on the road at one time, servicing reactive jobs. By using a CRM system, you have visibility of where your team members are and can assign the closest one to different jobs as they come in.

The CRM systems I would recommend checking out are Powered Now www.powerednow.com, Tradify www.tradifyhq.com/ simPRO www.simpro.co.uk and GeoOp www.geoop.com

Organisational

A **GANTT chart** is a simple tool that enables jobs to be managed more efficiently throughout a project schedule. Designed by Henry Gantt, an American mechanical engineer, a GANTT chart uses bar charts to represent the start and finish times of different elements of a project, enabling you to schedule, manage and monitor all the tasks and resources relating to it. The project timeline includes work scheduled and already completed over a particular time period.

This tool also enables other systems and processes to work efficiently, e.g. the ordering of materials and the management of staff to complete tasks on time. It enables staff to know what they have to do in what order, shows the tasks that can't be started until others are completed, and can identify and report any problems that occur along the way.

There are many GANTT chart tools widely available on the internet for a reasonable monthly fee, most of which offer free trials.

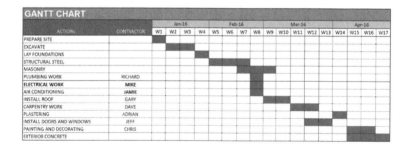

Time management is probably the most common problem I come across in working with Construction and Trades businesses. I often hear, 'I just don't have enough time' or 'How do I find the time to get everything done that I need to?' More often than not there is enough time; it is just not being managed effectively.

I have outlined below four different time management techniques that I have found to be helpful to clients. Everyone tends to have a favourite out of the four, so have a read through and choose the one that works best for you.

1. Urgent/important matrix. This is a tool created by US President Dwight D. Eisenhower and used by Stephen Covey, author of *The 7 Habits of Highly Effective People*. It is a simple way of organising your to-do list by prioritising the items on a basis of urgency and importance.

Urgent/important. These are tasks that you need to deal with within the next 24 hours and only you can **do** them, i.e. they can't be delegated.

Not urgent/important. These tasks are less urgent than above, i.e. they don't have to be done within the next 24 hours, but they are important and again can only be done by you. These should be **diarised**. Estimate how long the task is likely to take, and then block the time out in your diary.

Urgent/not important. These tasks could potentially be **delegated**, but need to be done fairly quickly. Challenge yourself and ask, 'Does this really need to be done by me?' Could it in fact be delegated to someone on the team or outsourced, e.g. invoicing, research, etc.?

Not urgent/not important. These are the sorts of things that may be taking up time, but add no value. It could be as simple as spending time on Facebook, surfing the internet, etc., or perhaps something that you have fallen into a habit of doing. **Ditch** these tasks.

2. The Ivy Lee method. Often referred to as the Six Most Important Things exercise. Charles Schwab, who was the President of Bethlehem Steel in 1918 and one of the richest men in the world at the time, brought in a productivity consultant named Ivy Lee to increase efficiency in his team. Schwab asked Lee how much it would cost for the advice and Lee famously said, 'Nothing.' He asked Schwab to pay him after three months what he thought his advice was worth. All he asked for was 15 minutes with each of the firm's executives.

When he met with the executives, Lee said, 'At the end of each day, write down the six most important things you need to get done tomorrow. List them in order of importance. When you come in to work tomorrow, start by focusing on the most important task, and when this is done move on to the next until they are all completed. At the end of the day, move any tasks that haven't been completed to the following day and repeat the process. Repeat this every day.'

After three months, Schwab was so delighted with the improvements Bethlehem Steel was making he wrote Lee a cheque for $25,000. At the time, the average worker in the US was paid $2 a day.

3. The £10, £100 and £1,000 task exercise. This is a technique that I was taught by one of my first mentors, Nick James, several years ago. Effectively, it gets you to think about the value of each of the tasks you have on your to-do list. It is a good way of challenging yourself in terms of whether you are holding on to too many low value tasks, and gets you to think about whether they could be delegated. It can also include the tasks that you would be doing if you had more time. Value is the amount of value a task creates for the business, as well as the cost that would be incurred if it were to go wrong. For business owners who are trying to do too much themselves, this is a great exercise to complete.

Below is a list of tasks that a client was doing himself, outlining how we allocated the value of each of them and the actions we took as a result:

Task	Complexity of task	Value	Action taken
Invoicing	Medium	Medium	Recruit office assistant to take care of this
Sending out quotes	Medium	Medium	Recruit office assistant to take care of this
Visiting prospective clients	Medium	High	Remains with business owner as this activity totally in line with his profile (see Chapter 2)
Working on site	Medium	High	Recruit some more subcontractors to free business owner to see prospective clients
Answering phone and email enquiries	Low	Medium	Recruit office assistant to take care of this
Researching different suppliers to ensure best value materials are being bought (we identified this wasn't happening at all)	Low	High	Delegate to a team member who has strengths in this area

Running around the area picking up materials that were needed for jobs but hadn't been ordered	Low	High	Reviewed the whole process as part of the customer journey and implemented a GANTT chart to ensure that all jobs were properly planned and all materials required ready on site for start date
Chasing payments of overdue invoices (we identified this was happening either not at all, ad hoc or a significant time after the due date)	Medium	High	Recruit office assistant to take care of this
Follow up calls to customer once job complete to conduct satisfaction survey (we identified this wasn't happening at all)	Medium	High	Recruit office assistant to take care of this and design customer feedback survey
Following up with customers when a service was due on their equipment (we identified that this was happening ad hoc, but was often significantly later than the due date)	Low	High	Recruit office assistant to take care of this
Visiting the team on site to monitor and provide feedback (this was happening, but again ad hoc and insufficiently)	Low	High	By freeing up his time through better delegation, the owner was able to divert more time to this valuable activity

4. Mind mapping. Mind mapping is a technique that has been used for thousands of years, but was made famous by British psychologist Tony Buzan. I find it an effective exercise to do when I have a large project to plan out that has many different elements.

Of our brain, 67% is visual, and therefore the brain likes it if we get everything out of our head and down on to paper in a visual format. A to-do list is linear and therefore not as effective, where as a mind map is far more memorable as it is in picture format.

To mind map, we start by entering the topic in the middle of the page and then we draw lines going off it to different related topics. I call these 'buckets'. We then draw lines off each bucket to identify all the elements relating to it. This can be an effective way of planning a job before completing a GANTT chart.

It might look like this:

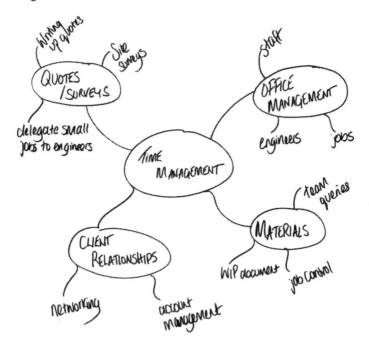

Unless you are taking time out to plan your week, it is likely that you will be in 'firefight' mode a lot of the time, reacting to whatever comes your way. If you are running your business this way, it is a bit like being in the passenger seat of a moving car. You are being taken wherever the driver goes, as opposed to deciding on the journey yourself.

Too many people are running their businesses this way, and it is a vicious circle. Until you take a step back and decide how you want to spend your time and how you are going to focus on the things that make a real difference to your business, you will never break this cycle.

Stephen Covey used to liken this to trying to fit large rocks in a bowl after lots of small rocks had been placed in there first. The large rocks are a metaphor for the important tasks – the tasks that will drive the business forward. Often these are the things about which business owners say, 'I'll get round to doing them one day', but never do. The small rocks relate to all the other things that take up your time, but don't add as much value and distract you from doing the things that will make a big difference.

We can see by the diagrams below that when we place the small rocks in first, there is no room for the big rocks. However, when we place the big rocks in first, the small rocks fit around them comfortably.

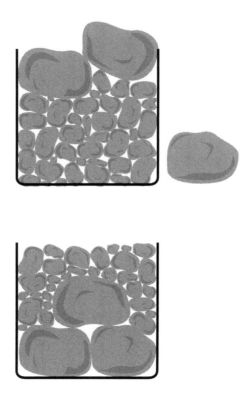

If you had to take a step back from your business, what things would you like to spend your time doing? These are likely to be the things that you are best at and enjoy the most. Don't worry about 'how' for the moment. Just imagine they're all possible and list them.

Planning the ideal week

I referred to Wealth Dynamics earlier and the different types of activities that energise us. We looked at Dynamo, Blaze, Tempo and Steel activities, so now let's look at what these activities could be in your business, and the importance of not constantly flitting from one type of task to the other. If we do so, it is tremendously tiring for our poor old brains, especially the prefrontal cortex which is required for thinking creatively.

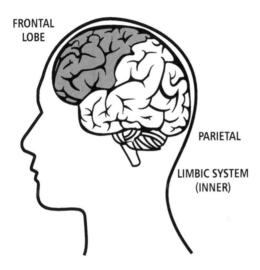

If you find that you are trying to concentrate on something and you just can't get into the task, it is likely that your prefrontal cortex is tired. One of the reasons may be that you are simply trying to do too many different types of tasks all on the same day.

Energy	Tasks
Dynamo	Creative tasks
Blaze	People based tasks, e.g. networking, client and team meetings
Tempo	Planning and organising
Steel	Detail orientated tasks, financial analysis, accounting tasks

When it comes to planning your ideal week, I would recommend the following:

Ensure you have an electronic diary, e.g. Outlook, that synchronises with your phone. This means that any updates or changes you make to your diary will synchronise immediately with the diary on your desktop as well as your phone. This may sound very basic, but I meet a number of Trades business owners who haven't got this in place and it causes havoc.

Ensure you block out time for different tasks each week, making sure that you don't have too many different types of task all on the same day.

The following is the weekly diary plan that we created for Jacques, who runs an air conditioning company employing three engineers and three subcontractors:

Day	AM	PM
Monday	Planning time (Tempo)	Review of the finances (Steel)
Tuesday	Seeing potential new clients (Tempo/Blaze)	Visiting sites to review progress of jobs (Blaze)
Wednesday	Office (Tempo/Steel)	Seeing potential new clients Tempo/Blaze)
Thursday	Networking meeting (Blaze)	Visiting sites to review progress of jobs (Blaze)
Friday	Seeing potential new clients (Tempo/Blaze)	Office (Tempo/Steel)

Jacques is a Deal Maker profile (see Chapter 2). He is most in flow seeing prospective and existing clients, winning the business and ensuring that the service meets or exceeds expectations. His strengths are closing new deals and providing great customer service.

As soon as we built the right structures to enable him to play more to his strengths, the customer service his company provided improved and as a result sales soared. Hence why you see more Tempo and Blaze activities – the key energies associated with a Deal Maker – in his diary.

CASE STUDY
Implementing systems and processes

Mark, whom I referred to earlier, came to see me initially in February 2016. He had been successfully growing his electrical business for the past few years, but felt at times like he was running the business 'on the back of fag packet'.

I knew his business well, and think he was being rather hard on himself. He was a good electrician and his company had a good reputation in the local area. However, there were definitely opportunities to make things run more smoothly and give Mark the sense of organisation he desperately wanted.

The following were the objectives, set by him, that he wanted to get out of the development programme:

- To achieve greater organisation (this was measured at a 5/10 at the beginning)
- To have a clear vision of the future and a plan of how to get there
- To develop a strategy to bring the right people in
- To be spending more time on the right things to drive the business

One of the most useful tools for him that he learnt about was the urgent/important matrix. He began using this every Monday to plan out his week and ensure that he was prioritising his tasks in the best way.

Here is what he had to say:

When I first started my electrical contracting business, my only concern was if I would have enough work. I concentrated on providing my clients with a first class service at a fair and competitive price, and within three years I had seven guys working for me. This is when I started to encounter problems I didn't anticipate. I was experiencing a high demand for my services and did not have the systems in place to deal with them. This resulted in me losing out on potential business and becoming very stressed. The biggest stress was that I had money coming in and going out, but had no visibility of what my company was earning and where our biggest expenses lay.

Mark said his three key challenges were:

Organisation – organising the guys on the job, sourcing materials, pricing work, my diary. Profitability was affected because the team didn't have the materials required, the level of service to clients was suffering, and I wasn't able to make meetings with potential new clients because I was caught up with dealing with issues.

Visibility of figures – I had no visibility of them really. We weren't getting regular P&L accounts, and when I did have them, it was a problem understanding them.

Knowing what to do because of the above, and who does what, as well as relinquishing responsibility to other people.

The things that Mark implemented that made a huge difference were:

- Having someone in the office
- Visibility of the figures – knowing what he was spending and earning each month and how to improve it
- Planning his week – he was reacting before
- Getting the right people doing the right job.

Team

It is very important that the team has a routine to work to and communication systems are in place to set the team up for success. Neil Gulvin runs a Health and Safety consultancy within the building industry and says it is so important to keep up to date files on each employee:

[Having] employees' personal development and training records ensures the organisation is training and developing

their employees and are a competent contractor. Employees benefit by having access to the file as this records all the employee's training and certification and gives the employee a sense of achievement and professionalism within the organisation.

One to ones are essential to keeping staff on track, but also for nipping problems in the bud that could potentially escalate. Dedicated time one on one with each employee each month over a coffee is time well spent. It shows you care about the individual enough to find out how things are going for them, and to provide them with some feedback.

Often employees may have the solution to a problem that you have been racking your brain to solve. Because they are closer to the coal front, so to speak, in a lot of cases, they often have good ideas and may have seen something that you have missed. One to ones therefore provide the opportunity for you to ask your staff what their opinion is about a particular problem and how they would go about solving it.

Often, I find poor communication causes a lot of a company's problems. Sometimes this is because the business owner doesn't have the right template to remind them about all the different elements of a job, e.g. when they're doing an initial site visit. Hence they don't collate all the right information to communicate back to the office. The business owner visits the customer and scribbles down key points on a bit of paper and then tries to remember all the different elements to prepare a full quote when they get back to the office. There are two problems with this: the business owner is carrying too much information around in their head, and they're not delegating the task of quote preparation. This creates a huge bottleneck, causing a delay. Customers chase for quotes, which puts the company in a bad light and often results in lost business.

This is exactly the situation that was occurring with the following client:

CASE STUDY
Defining roles and responsibilities

I was referred to Dave, the Managing Director of a construction company, in September 2016. He arrived for the consultation looking very stressed, but was also open to receiving help and advice.

We began working together in the October, and I could instantly see that the business would benefit from some simple structures to create better communication and enable Dave to let go of a lot of tasks.

Dave's strengths lay in creating fantastic conservatories. He was clearly talented and had a lovely way with customers. Winning the business was not the issue; it was what happened once he had agreed to send a quote that was where it was all going wrong.

Outlined below is the vicious circle he had found himself in:

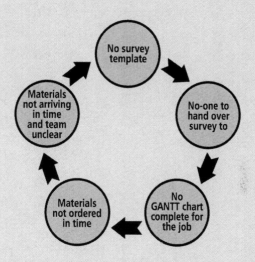

I could see by visiting the shop that there was no shortage of demand for Dave's services, but the sad fact was that most jobs did not go anywhere. Dave was physically unable to get all the estimates and quotes done, hence there was a ton of money being left on the table, so to speak.

This was a classic case of finding the 'plugs', as I call them, so the business would take off.

The steps we took were to:

- Defined roles and responsibilities so that Dave was able to let go of many of the tasks
- Appointed two team members as Project Manager and Logistics Manager
- Held a team meeting to outline the customer journey from enquiry to the point where the job started, highlighting the templates and process required
- Created effective survey templates, a basic one for the initial visit and a more comprehensive one for the full survey stage
- Created a GANTT chart so that the job could be properly planned, highlighting all the materials that were required
- Delegated responsibility for the ordering of the materials
- Implemented weekly team meetings so that the installers could be properly briefed on new and existing jobs

In addition to weekly meetings, monthly meetings including the whole team are also good practice for any business. The purpose for these is quite different to that of the weekly meetings, which are about briefing the team on the details of jobs for the following week.

Monthly meetings inform the team about:

- Company performance – sales, expenses and profit
- What has gone well over the month
- What could have been better over the month
- Rewarding and recognising anyone who has gone above and beyond.

Below are common challenges I hear when proposing the above, with my response including the benefits:

Challenge	Response
We simply haven't got the time to get the whole team together.	You will find that productivity increases because people are more motivated and less likely to make mistakes, so you will in fact have more time. Maybe start by having quarterly meetings and increase from there.
I don't think the team should be seeing how much money we are making.	I would challenge you to think about how you expect people to take ownership and care about the quality of their work if they are not aware how much things cost. Show trust in your people and it will be returned.
I don't see how sitting around in a room will change anything.	The team will be better informed, feel more valued and it will be far easier to hold them accountable.
It is impossible to physically get everyone together at the same time. We are too geographically spread out.	Nowadays, we don't all need to be in the same room to have a productive meeting. Online meeting software such as GoToMeeting or Zoom is very effective and everyone can join via their phones.

In summary, identify which systems and processes are missing from your company. What would make things run more smoothly? What could be automated, freeing up time for you and/or the team?

Try using one of the time management techniques and note the difference it makes to how organised and productive you become.

Chapter 4

LOVE YOUR CUSTOMER

In this chapter I will take you through the importance of measuring the customer experience that your company is providing, and how this can be a powerful driving factor if it is in the top 20% of your industry. In addition to taking you through ways of measuring the service, I have included a useful exercise called the 'Customer Journey', which is an excellent way of identifying bottlenecks in your business – those things that are actually capping the business's growth. Towards the end of the chapter is a detailed customer survey which you can put into a tool such as Survey Monkey to measure the experience provided by any Trades business.

The industry norm

The standard of customer service in the Construction and Trades industries often has lots of room to improve. This doesn't mean that the people who work within these industries are bad people or don't care. They mean well, and because of this they have no shortage of customers queuing up wanting to buy. However, they often over promise and under deliver.

Why? Well, in my experience it is because their businesses are more often than not out of balance, as discussed earlier in this book. What this looks like in the case of larger jobs is that someone, often the business owner – let's call him Bob, goes out to see the prospective client – we will call her Mrs Jones – when the initial enquiry comes in. All good so far. They build rapport, and Mrs Jones is keen to receive a quote.

This is where it begins to go wrong.

Bob goes back to his office and has several emails and phone calls concerning problems with other jobs to deal with. Mrs Jones's request for a quote is at best placed on his desk or logged in the filing cabinet – Bob's poor, overloaded brain. Sometimes Bob forgets completely, or wakes up in the middle of the night remembering that he hasn't got back to Mrs Jones. When he does, Mrs Jones may have found a different company to do the job. Or maybe she is still interested as she has had the same experience with other companies in the area.

Now there is a massive upside to this. It is easy to stand out as a good or even excellent business in this industry. Why? Because most businesses think that there isn't another way to work so they are not seeking help to change. The fact that you are reading this book puts you in the minority, and even if you implement just some of the things suggested here, you will stand a strong chance of delivering a better experience to your customers than that of your competitors.

Here are the top questions to ask yourself regarding customer service:

- Do you respond to customers in a timely manner/as quickly as you would like to?
- Do you and/or your staff always arrive on time for appointments with customers?
- Are you and your team smart in appearance?
- Do you appear to be organised?
- Do you follow up in a timely manner, e.g. sending out the quote, asking if the customer wants to proceed?
- How are the quality and timeliness of communication with customers, i.e. do you keep them informed?
- Do you always send out invoices on time?
- Do you and your team always leave the site clean and tidy?
- Are you and your team always polite, friendly and helpful?

The customer experience as a form of marketing

If you get the customer experience right, the opportunity is huge. Imagine that you had a defined process in place to:

- Deal with enquiries
- Produce a quote
- Follow up on the quote
- Win the job
- Order the materials
- Plan the staffing
- Complete the job on time and to budget
- Invoice the customer promptly

- Gather feedback from the customer to ensure they are happy

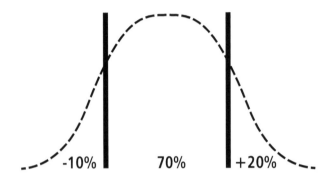

-10%   70%   +20%

Exercise. Think of all the companies that come to mind where you expect to receive bad service. Now think of all the companies that come to mind where you expect to receive excellent, reliable service.

You will probably find it easy to think of a company for both these scenarios, and it is likely that thinking of them is fairly emotive. You've had an appalling experience with one company that you could rant on about, and you've had an amazing experience with another that you could wax lyrical about. The common denominator is that both companies evoke emotion, and what happens when we feel emotional about something? We generally tell others. This is why it is very easy to gain a bad reputation, and is perhaps more challenging to gain an excellent reputation.

If you have the right systems and processes in place to provide an excellent customer experience, it is arguably easier to gain a place in the top 20% of Trades and Construction businesses than it is in other industries. If you move into this place and remain there, you will have more business than you know what to do with.

Often when clients initially come to me, they have been in the top 20%. They were providing excellent service in the beginning when it was just them in the business. Due to this, they were recommended, they grew, employed subcontractors or employees to help, and before they knew it, they were running a business. *But* they were still trying to do things as they had been before, and this is where it goes wrong.

In total there are 150,680 Trades businesses in the UK; Source: Analysis for Direct Line for Business. Competition is greatest in London, with there being only 131 households to every Trades business operating. This makes it even more important to ensure that your business is running like clockwork in this location, because if it isn't, there are plenty others for customers to choose from.

The Customer Journey

A great exercise to do for your business is one I have called the 'Customer Journey'. This involves mapping out each step the customer goes through as they come on board and experience the service.

The purpose of this exercise is to step into the customer's shoes so that you can experience the service they are receiving. It helps you think about what processes are potentially missing which would speed things up, or identify crucial information to communicate to other people in the team. For example, you may realise that a GANTT chart that outlines each step in a job will communicate your expectations to the team and help them do a better job.

The other reason for completing the Customer Journey exercise is that this is very effective at identifying bottlenecks in a business. This is where jobs are effectively held up at a particular stage, generally because the business owner is trying to do too much, and they simply haven't the time to keep everything moving.

CASE STUDY
Releasing the bottlenecks

Below is a flow diagram, which is how you can best map out a customer journey, showing what was revealed when I completed the Customer Journey exercise with a plumbing business owner, Rob:

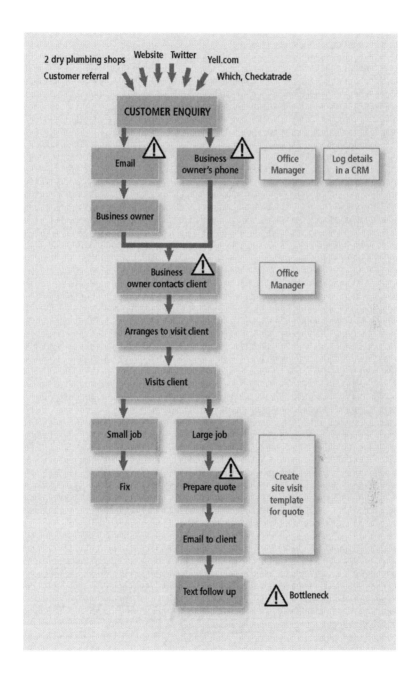

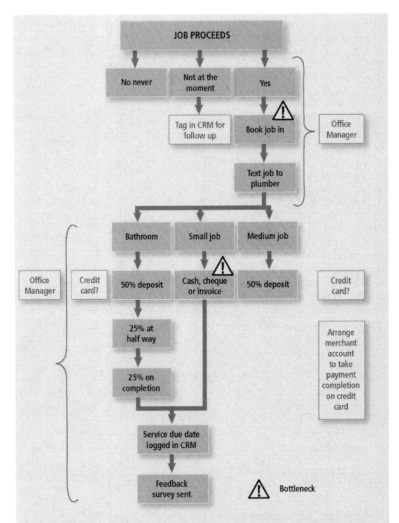

The text in black is what was happening, the text in grey is what we identified was needed for things to run more smoothly. The following are the bottlenecks that we identified, and on the right-hand side are the solutions we implemented:

Bottleneck	Problem	Solution	Benefit
All enquiries going to Rob, the business owner	Lots of enquiries not being responded to, work is lost	Part-time office assistant Outsource to Moneypenny	Rob can concentrate on seeing new customers and overseeing jobs Customer has a much more professional experience
No customer relationship management (CRM) system	Customer details not kept in one place, inability to market to them	CRM system specific to the industry	Efficiency Ability to send customers marketing literature
No quote template in place	Rob has to remember the information and write down on different pieces of paper. Stressful Difficult to remember details Onus on him to write it all down when back in the office	Quote template that is in electronic format to send immediately to office to communicate back to customer	All quotes are stored in one place in the CRM system Easy to retrieve Customer is communicated with far quicker
Jobs all booked in by Rob	Customers may not hear back straight away	Office assistant	Rob can concentrate on seeing new customers and overseeing jobs Customer has a much more professional experience
Deposits	Not always taken and no facility to take a credit card payment on the spot	Merchant account so credit cards can be taken	Cash flow is sped up

Customer doesn't want to proceed right now but will in the future	No record of the customer or their requirements, i.e. no pipeline strategy	CRM system Office assistant Follow up process	All potential customer enquiries are followed up
Payments	No process in place to take instalments	Office assistant manages this with the help of the CRM	Improved cash flow Professional customer experience
Servicing of boilers	No record of when servicing of customers' boilers is due	Office assistant manages this with the help of the CRM	Increased sales Professional customer experience
Customer feedback	No system in place to measure the customer experience	Customer survey created and submitted	Regular measurement and ability to respond quickly to any concerns/issues

The result of Rob implementing all the above was a sales increase of 54% and a profit increase of 50% after 12 months.

Exceed the client's expectations at the stage of:

Enquiry. This is arguably the most important stage, as we all know first impressions count. If you are answering the phone to a new customer while driving the van, going in and out of reception, they're hardly receiving the most professional of experiences. Furthermore, if you are trying to deal with enquiries, visit the customers, win the work, order the materials, do the work, invoice and chase the payments, it is likely you are going to burn out very soon.

Put yourself in the shoes of a customer. How would you like to be served? My guess is as professionally and efficiently as possible, which means that the phone needs to be answered promptly by someone in a quiet environment; someone who speaks clearly and confidently, is knowledgeable and can answer your questions.

Post-initial visit and quote. One of the best practices I came across in this industry was an electrician who knew that many of his potential customers would be getting other quotes. He made it part of his process to price up a job as soon as he got back in his van, then he would send the customer an email straight away. In it he would say that he'd enjoyed meeting them, he understood that they may be sourcing other quotes, and to please find attached a top tips booklet on the industry along with his quote.

He was able to provide the quote quickly in a lot of cases as he was using a CRM system specific to the industry, which he was able to access via his tablet. The booklet contained top tips to consider when sourcing an electrician, e.g. have you checked that they are insured? Do they have the necessary qualifications? Etc., etc. This did several things:

- It established him immediately as someone of credibility
- It contained genuinely useful, practical advice for the customer, which they appreciated
- It set him apart from the competition

- It built immediate trust
- It showed that he was professional and organised

Booking the job in. What do you need to inform the customer about when booking a job in? I would imagine that there are several common factors. Why not create a template to cover these, which can be used to ensure that all the necessary details are taken down? Not only does this mean that you and your team are set up for success when you arrive on site, but again it creates a professional, organised image.

How are we doing? So many times I ask a client how happy their customers are or how good the customer service they provide is. On most occasions, they tell me that they provide a great experience and there are no issues. Sometimes this is true, but unless they have a system in place that regularly measures the customer experience, it really is just their best guess, which is a dangerous place to be.

Customer surveys. These can be a great way of measuring your customers' experience, and if you have done a good job, they're also a great way of obtaining referrals to new customers. By using a free tool such as www.surveymonkey.net, you can create your own survey of up to 10 questions and send a link to all customers at the end of a job. This allows you to view all the feedback in one place and monitor trends, enabling you to respond quickly.

Below is an example of a customer survey template, which you can use in your business to fully assess strengths and weaknesses.

1. Please rate your overall experience on a scale of 1–10, with 10 being excellent, in the following areas:

	1	2	3	4	5	6	7	8	9	10
Friendliness										
Knowledge										
Helpfulness										
Responsiveness										
Communication										
Quality of work										
Tidiness										
Time keeping										
Value for money										

2. If you answered under 10 in any of the areas above, please can you tell us how we could have done better?

3. Which of the following services were you aware that we can provide? (List all your services in bullet point form for the customer to tick.)

4. Which of the following services would you be interested in knowing more about? (List the same services as above in bullet form.)

5. How happy were you with the service we provided at the different stages of the job?

	Not happy	Reasonably happy	Happy	Extremely happy
Initial contact				
Initial visit				
Producing the quote				
Quality of the job				
Post follow up				

6. If you answered less than happy to any of the above, please provide more detail.

7. Would you be happy to recommend our services to friends and family?

Yes

No (please provide details as to why)

8.   If you are happy to, please provide your details:

Name:

Email:

Phone number:

My recommendations are that you set up all of the questions to require an answer, apart from question eight, which asks for the customers' details. I would also ensure that question eight is the last question that you ask. The reason for this is that people will have already answered the questions, so they are more likely to submit the survey. If the survey asked for their details at the beginning, it could put them off completing it.

Whether or not you ask for customers' details carries pros and cons. If you ask for their details and make this compulsory, people may either not bother or not tell you the whole truth. If you don't ask for their details, you have no way of knowing whom to go back to should you wish to. Over the years I have decided that it is best to ask, but allow this to be optional and then you have all areas covered.

Mystery shopping. This is a great way of obtaining truly objective feedback, as the whole visit is conducted by a specialist company such as Shoppers Anonymous www.shoppersanonymous.co.uk.

You receive a full report on different aspects of the customer journey and an overall score.

In summary, we have established that within the Construction and Trades industries there is arguably more opportunity to stand out from the competition by providing great customer service. By completing the Customer Journey exercise, you are able to identify bottlenecks and processes that are missing which are preventing the work from flowing. Remember to measure the customer experience you are providing regularly so that you can continually improve the process and respond to any issues.

Think about implementing the following into your business to measure and improve the service you are providing:

- Continually measure the service using a survey and an online tool such as Survey Monkey to establish trends
- Create a Customer Journey flow chart to show what is happening currently
- Identify bottlenecks and in a different colour show what the ideal journey would look like
- Use an external provider to conduct mystery shop visits at least once a quarter to get truly objective feedback on your service experience

Chapter 5

DEVELOP AND DELEGATE –
HIRING GOOD EMPLOYEES

In this chapter, I will take you through some best practices to ensure that you attract, select and retain good people.

In the Trades and Construction industries I see a lot of what we call 'panic hiring'. This is where the business owner finds themselves in desperate need of someone, the next-door neighbour's best friend has a son who is looking for a job and has done something similar in the past, and hey presto! After meeting for a coffee and a chat, the business owner hires him.

Taking someone into your business is probably the most crucial decision you will ever make. This may sound dramatic, but this person will be representing your company and its image by serving your customers, possibly coming into contact with them more often than you do. Therefore it is imperative that they are good. Not to mention their reliability and whether or not they can actually do the job.

Panic hiring causes a whole load of problems. The biggest mistakes I see are:

- Only having one candidate to see
- Not thinking about what is important in terms of skills and attitude

- Recruiting people with the wrong attitude
- Not advertising the role so that you have several candidates to choose from
- Rushing the selection process
- Not having a selection process

Finding the right employee

'Where do I find good people?'

This is possibly one of the most common questions asked of me by clients and is arguably the biggest challenge for any business owner, including those in the trades. People who are both capable and have a good attitude can be hard to come by, so when you find them, you need to keep them.

Employer branding is essentially thinking of your company as a brand for employees as opposed to customers. In other words, how attractive does your company look in terms of a prospective workplace? All of the following need to be considered:

The website – does the website have a careers section? Does it have a section covering what it is like to work for you? If you have a set of company values, are they on there?

Many Trades businesses don't have any of this, so it is easy to stand out as an employer of choice by taking these simple steps.

The job advert – be truthful. Don't try and make the company sound something that it isn't. It is important that there is consistency between what you describe and what the applicant sees.

The recruitment process – remember that this is a two-way process. The applicant is forming opinions about what it might be like to work for you and how professional you appear. If you have high standards yourself, this sets the bar and an expectation of what you are looking for in an employee.

The reality of working for you – in a similar way to the job advert, don't try and sell applicants an apple and give them a pear. What you tell them about the company during the selection process needs to match the reality of working there. If there are challenges, be honest and tell them in as nice a way as possible.

Recruitment is not an exact science, but we can do several simple things to make the chances of hiring someone good far more likely. Here are my basic top tips:

Plan ahead. Don't fall into the trap of waiting till you need someone before starting to look.

Know what you are looking for – skillsets and attitude. Put some time into thinking about this, and it will be time well spent. You can download an example of a job description from our website here: www.evolveandgrowcoaching.com/book-downloads

Ask around. This can be a valuable exercise, as employees who are recommended to you are more likely to be good. Just make sure that you have several people to choose from as opposed to one or two.

Advertise the role. I would recommend using job boards as opposed to the local paper, which is rather outdated now. If people are looking for a job they will usually look online. A company such as Hiring People www.hiringpeople.co.uk is worth using, as you can purchase a package at a competitive price which gets your advert on all the major job boards, including Jobsite www.jobsite.com which is good for Trades. Hiring People will also help you structure the ad in such a way that it is more likely to be found through a search online.

Ask for a CV with applications. I know that not all tradespeople have CVs, and that is the point. Only those who are serious about applying and really want the job will go to the trouble to put one together.

Look for gaps between jobs and how long applicants have stayed in jobs. This can be a good indication of how reliable they are and how long they are likely to stay. Long gaps between jobs could indicate that they have either walked out or been dismissed. During a telephone interview be sure to ask about any gaps.

Conduct a telephone interview. A lot of time can be saved by telephone interviewing applicants. These interviews should last no longer than 15 minutes and will give you the basic information you need in order to decide if applicants are worth meeting face to face. (See suggested telephone interview questions later in this chapter.)

You can download a free telephone interview from our website here www.evolveandgrowcoaching.com/book-downloads

Consider using psychometric testing. Psychometrics are online tests that you can ask applicants to complete to give you an indication of their strengths. I would certainly recommend using these for office/admin roles. There are two types. **Ability tests** normally involve verbal and numerical reasoning. These give an indication of how quickly the applicant is likely to hit the ground running. **Personality tests** give you an indication of their strengths and weaknesses and how likely they are to enjoy the role and therefore stay.

Include a practical assessment. With Trades positions I would recommend including some form of supervised practical assessment to see how skilled applicants are at the job.

Conduct face to face interviews with those shortlisted from telephone interviews. This is not just a coffee and a chat. Make sure that you ask questions about their past experience where they have to give you examples. Download a competency based interview from our website here www.evolveandgrowcoaching.com/book-downloads.

Check references. I would advise asking for details of the applicant's two most recent employers, and carry reference checking out over the phone. Often written references will only confirm that they were employed and the dates. You can glean a lot more by speaking to their previous employers, who are more likely to be open about what they were really like on the phone.

Keep the details of any good applicants you don't employ. Let's imagine that you have three good people you could offer the job to, but you can only afford to take one on. This is a great position to be in, but make sure that you stay in touch with the two who aren't taken on. Next time you need someone, you already have their details and hopefully won't need to go through the whole process again.

I am aware that the above may seem very corporate and alien to tradespeople. But trust me – by applying these best practices, you will save yourself many headaches down the line as you are far more likely to find good people. Good people turn up on time, do a good job, think for themselves, don't give you grief, take responsibility, etc., etc.

CASE STUDY
Implementing people systems and processes

Kris came to me in 2014 with a successful painting and decorating business. He was known in the area as providing excellent quality on time and value for money service, and had begun to franchise the model. He had two franchisees already in place, but wanted help with processes to grow this side of the business. One such process was recruitment.

Kris's approach to recruitment was very much 'suck it and see' and this was causing him a certain amount of stress. He would recruit people first as an employee, and if they were good, he'd offer them a franchise. Nothing especially wrong with this, but more often than not they didn't work out and caused him a fair few problems in the process.

Firstly we implemented a few processes on the people side of the business to improve the chances of him finding good employees who could then become franchisees. We also put some other processes in place that helped him measure their performance and develop them – but more of that later.

Three years on and Kris now has five franchisees on his books and the business is thriving. He says when asked about recruitment:

It actually worked so well I haven't done much of it recently, as I have kept the same team for a year; I have the right people. I haven't advertised for staff for at least a year now. Before I was advertising for every new job, getting rid of one lot and getting a new lot on board.

CASE STUDY
Building the right team

Roland, whom I referred to earlier in the book, runs a successful window cleaning company. He learnt to adapt the principles outlined here to focus on identifying the right attitude, which is crucial in this industry.

He says the following:

Attitude towards the work is difficult to assess at recruitment stage. I ask them about previous work and the ones who are not right will generally complain a lot about their jobs. I will ask them how previous jobs were and they tell me they didn't work out. This together with a training day gives me a pretty good picture. I have to accept then that they won't always do the job the way I do. It's not their business, not their baby. They will do it well enough for the customer, but I myself would give that bit extra, which they wouldn't.

You have to keep looking for the right people. If someone lacks something, find someone else who is better, but you will never find someone who is the same as you. You have to decide which bits you are willing to compromise on.

Example of a job ad:

Heating Engineer, South East London – Salary Competitive

NB: Please note only applications who include a CV will be considered.

Pipedream Plumbers is a leading provider of installation and heating services to the domestic and commercial markets, based in Bromley, South London, covering **South London and North Kent.**

We have an exciting opportunity for an experienced gas-safe engineer to join our **friendly family based** firm.

This is an ideal opportunity for someone who is **looking to join a company where they can develop their career** and benefit from working under the name of a **respected established brand.**

We pride ourselves in providing **exemplary customer service**, and only engage with individuals who reach our **high expectations**.

It is essential that successful applicants can demonstrate a **strong commitment to the customer**, as well as **trustworthy** and **reliable** behaviours.

Essential requirements:

- Your own set of tools
- An ability to demonstrate a strong track record as a fully competent gas-safe engineer
- Full clean driving licence
- Good communication skills.

We offer an extremely **competitive rate of pay**, 20 days paid holiday a year and a profit share scheme.

This advert may sound over the top to you and that is a good thing. This template has been used for a variety of my clients across different Trades industries. Because it sounds the way it does, it deters the mediocre candidates from applying and attracts people who take their job seriously and want to work for a well-run company. Set the bar high, and this is what you will attract. Remember we are aiming to be in the top 20% in order to turn our customer base into our marketing (see Chapter 4).

Example of a telephone interview script (download here): www.evolveandgrowcoaching.com/book-downloads

Question	What you are looking for when asking this
What are you doing at the moment?	What skills do they have which are needed in the position that you have?
What have you done in the past?	Do they switch between completely different jobs? This could show that they haven't really found what they want to do.
Why are you looking for a new job?	Is it for career progression or are they unhappy? If they are unhappy, what is it that is making them so?
What do you enjoy about your job?	You obviously want someone who enjoys their job as opposed to someone who just needs a job.
What don't you enjoy about your job?	All of us probably have aspects of our jobs we don't enjoy, but these shouldn't be the main parts of the job.
How would your best friend describe you?	This is one that can catch people slightly, and you can therefore get a true response as opposed to the 'right' answer.
Can you think of the last time you let your employer down? What were the circumstances and how did you manage the situation?	Again this can catch people off guard and you are therefore more likely to get the truth. If someone tells you they have never let anyone down, they are probably lying!
When did you last have to make a difficult decision? What did you do?	This gives an indication of how they make decisions and whether they take action.

When have you had to deal with a difficult customer? What did you do?	This shows you how they deal with complaints and issues. Are they likely to calm situations down and resolve problems?
Where do you see yourself in five years' time?	A bit of a cliché, but this can give you an indication of their level of ambition and how serious they are about the job.

Bringing employees on board

It amazes me how many business owners do not have simple basics in place to set both the employee and the business up for success. I covered some of these in Chapter 3, but in the remainder of this chapter I will go into more detail around what these basics are, which will greatly improve the chances of you developing and keeping good quality people.

I have worked closely for several years with a local firm, Achor Employment Law. I have frequently put clients in touch with the founder, Esther Fagbemiro, when they have got into tricky situations with their employees. Seldom have they had the right documents in place, which doesn't bode well and can be costly both in time and money to rectify.

One of the most important documents is a contract. Here is what Esther has to say regarding subcontractors, who many business owners may think do not require one:

Having a written contract between your business and the self-employed contractors that you engage is crucial and sensible. Putting things in writing is not a trap and does not give the contractor more rights than you want them to have. There are some clauses that you should include so that your contract is in line with legal requirements and established practice, but there is still room for you to make it bespoke for your needs.

For example, a written contract will set out what you expect from the contractor, and what the contractor can expect from you in exchange for providing the service(s).

Importantly a written contract should set out and make clear:

- *The contractor's responsibility for meeting tax liabilities to HMRC*
- *The contractor's responsibility for having adequate and correct insurances in place from reputable providers*
- *The employment status of the contractor, for example a 'No employment' clause*

[These are examples only, there are other clauses that should be included to meet legal requirements.]

A contract can be written, verbal or develop as a matter of custom and practice over time. However, a written contract is the best way to ensure that both parties to the relationship are clear about their rights and obligations. Also, a written contract is a superior and reliable source of evidence if a dispute ever develops between you and the contractor, or indeed you and a client.

To read more about UK Employment Law and Esther's organisation please visit http://www.achoremploymentlaw.co.uk/.

Inducting the new employee. This is another time where companies, and not just Trades, often fall down. Imagine how you might be feeling starting a new job. Whenever we enter into the unknown, there is bound to be a certain amount of doubt and fear associated with it. The first 90 days in any new role are critical, and lots of studies have been conducted showing the link between their experience in those first 90 days and how likely a person is to stay and perform.

Here are my top eight things to implement when a new person starts:

- Issue a contract
- Set expectations
- Ask them what their expectations are
- Introduce them to the team
- Give them a buddy

- Stress the importance of timekeeping and reliability
- Let them know how they will be paid and what you need from them
- Outline current projects/workload

In summary, you always need to be planning ahead and willing to meet with potentially good employees or subcontractors. The worst thing a business can do is panic hire, as invariably it leads to problems further down the line.

If a proper process is planned and applied to each step, you will be far more likely to hire someone who is skilled, has the right attitude and stays with you. This means:

- Advertising the role using a well-worded advertisement
- Having several candidates to choose from, not just one
- Ensuring that each candidate has been telephone screened, had a face to face interview and undergone some form of practical assessment
- Planning new employees' induction, not just throwing them in at the deep end

Chapter 6

DEVELOP AND DELEGATE –
KEEPING EMPLOYEES

In this chapter we look at best practice to follow once you have hired and brought on board a new member of the team. This all about developing and keeping them so you are not continuously going through the cycle of recruiting, training and replacing.

Here is my list of top things to do which will pay dividends:

Meet each employee for a 121 on a regular basis. This should be a minimum of once a quarter and enable you to provide employees with positive and constructive feedback, while they give you feedback around how they feel and any improvements that could be made. By sticking to this discipline, you will find any niggling problems can be nipped in the bud and prevented from going pear-shaped.

Have a monthly team meeting. This is a great way to share what is going well and what needs to be improved, including any problems that keep occurring. By sharing problems with the team and asking them what ideas they have that could help resolve them, you could find the perfect solution to a problem, and if the team comes up with the solution, they are far more likely to implement it. So even when you have the answer, it is sometimes worthwhile to ask the team anyway. If they come up with the same solution, they will think it was their idea and will be more likely to follow through. There is so much psychology involved in managing people.

Share how the company is doing. I frequently work with business owners who are nervous about sharing the company performance with their team. They somehow feel the employees will make judgments which will negatively affect their attitude. I actually think it has the opposite effect: they feel valued that you trust them with this information and are more likely to take responsibility when they see how much things cost. In addition, they see the targets the company is aiming for and how their performance can contribute to them.

Share what has gone well on jobs, and what hasn't. Again, by involving the team and taking the time to communicate with them, you send out a message that they are valued and their opinions count.

I was working recently with a team of installers in a construction company who had created the ideal process from an enquiry coming in to the job being booked. I had actually already gone over processes with the business owner, but the process the team created was quite different and far more aligned with what was needed. They were closer to the day to day and could see where things were falling down, hence the new customer journey process was a better fit for purpose and they felt great that they had been asked.

Ask them for their opinion. I'm sure you're getting an idea of what I am saying now – show people that you respect them and value their opinion and they will be far more likely to strive to do their best, take ownership and make sensible decisions. Someone once told me a long time ago that too many line managers, and this is across all industries, treat their people like mushrooms, i.e. keep them in the dark and feed them dirt, and then wonder why people don't do a good job.

Share your vision of the company. Tell people where you are going, or even better, ask them what they would like to see and create the vision together. Imagine working for an employer whose plans you didn't know and the only time they spoke to you was to tell you when you were doing something wrong. You wouldn't feel part of something or see what difference it made if you did a good job or a bad job. Would you be bouncing out of bed in the morning to go to work? I'd guess not.

If you have company values, refer to them frequently. Company values state what you stand for. They are your beliefs around how work should be done, customers served and staff treated. In other words, they represent your culture.

Company values can be seen as corporate jargon that doesn't mean anything, and in a lot of cases they don't. This is not because the values don't work; it is because many organisations pay lip service to them. They sit somewhere on a shelf, or maybe they are on the wall of reception, but the employees are certainly not living and breathing them.

It is how companies choose to use their values that make the difference, and they can be a nice addition to the 'What Good Looks Like' document. In the Construction and Trades industries, because company values are rare, they can really help you stand out from your competition – providing that you live up to them.

Here is an example of Command Electricals' values. They are on the company's website and frequently referred to by Mark, the business owner.

Care about the details. We're the Rolls Royce of electricians. We care for the work we do, how we do it and the impact on the customer.

Professional with personality. We run like a big business – organised, focused and professional, but think outside of the box. We have character and charm. And fun along the way.

Quality is king. The service we give and the work we do is always better than the rest. We put our customers first and deliver value. We live up to our reputation – every time.

Doing it together. Whether it's as a team or with our customers, we work as a partnership. It's all about win-win.

Always with integrity. Trust, honesty and respect – the foundations on which we are built.

Mark says this when asked how having values has helped:

> *They have helped the team because they can see what we are about. They help us give better service to the clients, as they set the level that we need to work to. If there is an incidence when things are not up to scratch, they act as a point of reference. Customers have commented on them, and have been surprised to see them on our website as it is quite rare in the trades to have them. It is what people want to see.*

Give encouraging feedback. Always try to give three times as many positive messages to negative. This is proven to be the right ratio when it comes to improving the performance of your team. If people hear two positive messages vs one negative, they probably only hear the negative and nothing will change. If they hear more than three to one, it has been found that they see the feedback as being insincere and it loses its effectiveness. Feedback can be as simple as a thank you for a job well done, or an enquiry as to how they are, as long as it is genuine.

Position constructive (negative) feedback in a positive way. The language you use is very important. If I say to you, 'In all these areas there isn't a problem, *but* you really need to make sure you do X, Y and Z', it is likely that you will go away feeling pretty demotivated. However, if I say to you, 'I think you are doing really well in these areas, *and* what I would like to see you doing is X, Y and Z', would this make you feel differently? The subtle use of *and* as opposed to *but* is part of it, but also the fact that I am asking to see something as opposed to saying what is wrong also positions the conversation differently.

Ultimately if you want an employee to change their behaviour, you need to ensure they feel positive for this to happen. Don't get me wrong – if something is a serious issue, that requires a different type of conversation, but if it is just general improvements that they need to make, this is the best way to approach it.

Conduct annual appraisals. These are a good way of consolidating all your feedback from the previous year and finding out the aspirations of your staff. It may be that someone would like to develop and take on more responsibility, but if you don't take the time out to ask, you may never know.

In the Construction and Trades industries, like many others, employees are far more loyal to you as their employer if you develop and promote people to a position of responsibility internally as opposed to externally.

I am fully aware that all of the above looks like hard work, and it is. However, it is not nearly as hard as having poor performing employees who are unreliable, don't care, turn up late, make mistakes, don't take ownership, etc., etc. Take a moment to think how much of your time is taken up, not to mention the cost incurred, by all of the aspects I have just listed. You can probably double that, as all these things cause considerable knock on effects in your business.

Imagine that by implementing these best practices, you create a high performing team of engaged individuals who take ownership and think for themselves, almost showing as much care for the company as they would if it was their own. The knock on effects of this type of workforce give you back so much – time, less stress, space to think, etc., etc.

Expectation setting

Most large organisations have competency frameworks. These are like internal bibles and clearly set out the behavioural expectations required. This may sound very corporate and far too formal for a small business, but I would encourage you to think of these practices as the oil in the engine. We all know what happens if we don't service our car and ensure it has all it needs, e.g. oil, water, etc., to enable it to run well – it grinds to a halt and breaks down.

Think of running a business like running a well-oiled machine. What are the tasks that you can do religiously, day in day out, week in week out, month in month out, that are habits and ensure that the business runs well?

Let me tell you what I often see happening: business owners are frustrated with their staff, mainly due to them not doing something in the right way, not thinking for themselves, not showing initiative, or not being reliable. I then discover in the majority of cases that clear behavioural expectations have never been set. This is different from the technical skills that business owners expect. Someone can be a technically skilled electrician, for example, but if they don't use their initiative, leave the work area in a mess, and frequently turn up late for work, I would imagine they are a bit of a headache.

So this is the reason why I would strongly recommend you have a version of the corporate competency framework in your business. Let's call it a 'What Good Looks Like' document for now. This will help you to:

- Hire the right people
- Have good, reliable staff
- Keep and develop the best staff
- Have fewer people problems
- Free up your time to work on other things

Let's look at an example of such a document (this form can be downloaded from our website via this link): www.evolveand growcoaching.com/book-downloads

The broad areas of competency are:

- Customer Focus
- Results Focus
- Teamwork
- Ownership and Decision Making
- Communication

Customer focus	1	2	3
Is always professionally dressed and looks smart			
Keeps the site clean at all times			
Demonstrates care towards the customer's property and possessions			
Is punctual and reliable			
Communicates any delays immediately			
Is professional and courteous at all times with customers			
Can take complaints and criticism without getting emotional or taking it personally			
Responds to messages from customers and management promptly			
Is prepared to go above and beyond to do what is right for the customer			

Results focus	1	2	3
Follows instructions and when appropriate raises issues with line manager			
Approaches their work in a methodical manner, ensuring that correct preparation is undertaken			
Demonstrates an ability to plan all jobs well so that they are done in the most efficient way			
Completes jobs within realistic timelines and without compromising on the quality of work			
Has excellent attention to detail, always strives to do a good job			
Demonstrates an eagerness to learn and continuously improve			
Maintains level of commitment consistently, ensuring job is completed to standard			
Sees mistakes as an opportunity to improve			

Teamwork	1	2	3
Builds good, effective working relationships with other team members			
Takes an interest in other team members' activities in regards to both productivity and health and safety			
Works effectively as part of a team, helping others when necessary			
Works with the team to ensure that they meet deadlines			

	1	2	3
Is supportive of their colleagues, approachable and responsive			
Is not afraid of talking to other team members in the right way if they are not performing or carrying out instructions			
Calms down heated situations			
Willing to take instructions from peers when necessary			

Ownership and decision making	1	2	3
Takes full ownership for their work and avoids blaming others			
Is reliable and punctual			
Takes the time to think of an appropriate solution to a problem			
Deals with unexpected circumstances in a logical manner and takes responsibility for them			
Approaches problems in a calm, effective manner, not afraid of making a mistake			
Gets the job done within the agreed timelines, takes ownership and goes beyond if necessary			
Reviews and reassesses plans and priorities on a regular basis			
Does not procrastinate; makes quick, effective decisions			

Communication	1	2	3
Communicates respectfully and effectively with other team members			
When circumstances change, communicates to line manager and/or customer			
Is appropriately assertive and confident without upsetting the customer			
Diffuses tension when faced with an angry or anxious customer			
Communicates with the customer during each job and upon completion to ensure that they are informed and happy			
Listens actively and attentively			
Uses appropriate method of communication to match the situation, e.g. phone, text or email			
Updates and informs line manager appropriately			

1 = Below expectations
2 = Meets expectations
3 = Exceeds expectations

This document can be used in 121 meetings and annual appraisals to communicate to someone where they are doing well and where you would like to see them improve.

Ask the staff member to score where they think they are on each of the behaviours prior to sitting down with them, and you do the same. This will give you an indication of how aware they are about their performance, and because it is down in black and white, they can see that these are the expectations you have of all employees and you are not singling them out in any way.

At the recruitment stage ask for examples of when an employee has demonstrated certain behaviours. This is far more powerful than asking what they would do in a certain situation because it is fairly easy to make something up. Most of us know what we should do, but we want to know what employees have done. (You can download a competency based interview for trades on my website via the link.)

Induction. Have your 'What Good Looks Like' document made into a small brochure for staff to take away with them on their first day and have a read through. It is also a good idea to go through this with them, explaining anything that might not be clear. All of this is what I call due diligence, best practice or the oil that makes the machine run well. If you take the time to do this right at the beginning of someone's employment, you are far less likely to have headaches further down the line.

One to one meetings. I would recommend that at least once a quarter, you sit down with each team member for a 121. This can be done in the café or even at the pub. If anything, doing it in this kind of environment will make it more relaxed and the conversation will flow. Refer to the 'What Good Looks Like' document when giving both constructive and positive feedback to reinforce expectations.

Annual appraisals. If you have been doing regular 121s with your staff, the annual appraisal meeting should be easy. So often I work with business owners who don't stick to the 121s and then tell their employee something that has been bothering them in the annual appraisal. This is never the time to give someone a piece of constructive feedback for the first time. The annual appraisal is simply a summary of everything you have been talking about during the year.

Coaching vs telling. Frequently I come across frustrated business owners who complain of staff not thinking for themselves, not being proactive and generally causing them problems. I usually find that this is due to the business owner not letting go and allowing their team to take ownership of issues. They rush in to solve things, taking control, often overriding their team. This causes many problems, including the team not feeling valued, trusted or respected. They are therefore unlikely to think for themselves, always looking to their boss for answers, and the cycle continues.

Most business owners in the industry have never been coached how to lead a team or get the best out of people, so this cycle is hardly any surprise. It would be a bit like me going to install electrics in a house or fix a leaky tap. I have never been shown how to.

I have listed below examples of the telling vs the coaching approach against a couple of common problems. I would encourage you to try using the coaching questions, especially in a 121, and see the different response you get from your team.

In the following situations, Alan is the owner of a plumbing business and Rob is the staff member.

Situation. Rob is continually making mistakes.

Telling. A: 'I need you to pay more attention, I can't keep having these mistakes made.'

R: 'OK, fine.'

Coaching. A: 'We need to ensure that these mistakes are fewer, can you tell me what might be the reason behind why you are making them?'

R: 'I'm not sure, maybe I need more training.'

A: 'Training in what specifically?'

R: 'I don't feel completely confident in installing a boiler, it would be good to cover that again.'

A: 'OK, how about I put you with Carl next week? He is very good at installing boilers and can answer any questions you have.'

Let's look at a different situation.

Situation. Alan has had some feedback that Rob was not very helpful with a customer.

Telling. A: 'Rob, Mrs Jones commented to me the other day that you were not very helpful when she asked for additional work to be done. I can't have this happening in the business, next time please make sure you appear more helpful.'

R: 'I don't think I was unhelpful. She was asking for something that we hadn't planned into the day, we wouldn't have been able to get it all done.'

A: 'Look, we have spoken about this before, Rob. I don't need this hassle, just make sure that next time you do what they are asking, alright?'

R: 'Fine.'

Coaching. A: 'Rob, Mrs Jones commented to me the other day that you were not very helpful when she asked for additional work to be done. Can you tell me a little bit more about what happened?'

R: 'Yes, it was 4.30pm and she asked me to look at her toilet that she thought was leaking. I had to leave at 5pm and she hadn't mentioned it before.'

A: 'How do you think that may have come across?'

R: 'Well I guess it may have appeared a bit unhelpful, but I don't know what else I could have done. I had to leave at 5pm to go and collect my daughter.'

A: 'What could you have done?'

R: 'I'm not sure.'

A: 'Well, I get that you had to leave at 5pm, but we also have our company image to think about.'

R: 'I know, I didn't mean to appear unhelpful.'

A: 'I'm sure you didn't, so perhaps have a think about if this was your business, how would you have dealt with it?'

R: 'I could have offered to come back the following day to have a look at it, explaining that I didn't have time today and would want to ensure that I properly investigated it.'

A: 'Great, that would have meant that we appeared helpful, and of course we may have ended up with some more business.'

This may seem 'fluffy', and you may be thinking you haven't got the time to be doing all this coaching stuff. You may also be thinking your staff just need to do their job or you'll get someone else. The choice, of course, is yours, but if you are finding yourself saying the same things over and over like a parrot without seeing any improvements, I would encourage you to try this approach.

In a nutshell, taking a coaching approach fosters many good behaviours. Your team members will think for themselves, which means that they are taking a form of ownership of a problem. You are asking them to identify the solution which may be a better solution than you would have thought of, and they are more likely to own it as they have come up with it. Over time, people will learn to think for themselves and come up with solutions to every problem they encounter rather than referring to you the whole time. This approach therefore builds confidence in the team and they feel trusted, which in turn creates a workforce that is more likely to enjoy their job and stay.

Take the time to coach, even if it is more time consuming in the short-term. It will definitely save time in the long-term and you will have a more capable, engaged workforce in the process.

Not letting go

Letting go is often the biggest challenge for any business owner, regardless of the industry they are in. When you have built a business from scratch, it is your baby and your name above the door, so to speak. However, if you don't learn to let go, you will never be able to grow and expand, and you may burn yourself out. I have seen many people make themselves ill trying to control everything.

Jacques of JP Air Conditioning says:

> *It was tough to let go of the engineers and worrying about if they would complete jobs properly. I trained Carlos well in our standards, so he would update me on a daily basis on what was happening. You need to have people you can trust – a right hand person, and give them a role to be this. Carlos often says to me that we have grown this business together; he is a proud member of the team.*

This is a great example of how Jacques put someone he trusted implicitly in place to effectively be his 'eyes and ears'. This gave him a degree of comfort that jobs were being completed to standard even when he was not there.

For Kris Jamroz of Brush Strokes Decorating, it was about having the systems and processes in place to identify the right people at the recruitment stage. This gave him the confidence to let go.

He says:

> *The funny thing was that one thing followed the other which started with attracting the right people, and*

because I could trust them more, I didn't have to spend as much time managing them, and the business generally went better. A better workforce resulted in fewer problems and better relationships with clients, and the time spent with them was constructive rather than focused on problems. I am no longer a painter whose task is to paint a wall, I am a business partner for my main contractors.

Mark from Command Electrical previously felt that unless he was on the tools earning money, he wasn't doing a day's work. He began to realise that as the MD of a company, he couldn't hold on to everything if he wanted to grow.

He told me:

There is only one of me in the business. I can't get bogged down with making minor decisions, I have to let the guys do this with guidance. The time I have spent on minor decisions in the past wasn't right. It's so nice now as there are conversations going on in my company that I don't know about because the people I have in place know their role, e.g. on Friday we couldn't use a certain material on the job and the problem was reported, solved and rectified without me even knowing, which was great! I could never have envisaged that before, everything had to come through me.

You don't have to be physically doing the work to be a company asset. In this industry it is all about being practical and working hard, but the time and money that can be saved from getting the back office working is huge.

We have looked at the importance of having clear expectations in place and some tools and processes that can help reinforce these. Take the time to advertise for vacancies so that you have more than one candidate to choose from, have regular chats with employees and provide them with positive and constructive feedback. Your business will only ever be as good as the people you employ, as they relate directly to the service you provide and your ability to step back and run the business.

INTERVIEW WITH LEV FEVZI
SMART SECURITY SERVICES

I met Lev, an owner of a security business, earlier this year through BNI. He belongs to another local Chapter and was covering for a member of our Chapter when I got chatting to him after a meeting.

I noticed that he was walking with a stick. It transpired that he had been in a serious accident a year earlier and had almost lost his leg. What he told me next, however, was far more shocking – he said that the accident had been 'a blessing' as it had forced him to move from working 'in his business' to working 'on it'.

This is his story.

Before the accident I was feeling I couldn't trust anyone to do my job, although I worked with many people who were very capable. I would come home and do all the admin, invoicing and trying to get new clients. I was probably doing a 20-hour day most days and I was shattered. I was trying to be in three places at once and please every single client.

In addition to running the business, I had to work part-time for someone else to make enough money. I was on my way to that job that day – that tragic day, as some people would call it, but I call it a blessed day.

I had the accident at 5.05pm on 22 April 2016. A van driver decided to run me over when I was on my motorbike, snapping my femur bone, breaking my shoulder and right foot. I was on the side of the road for two hours while paramedics stabilised me. I got airlifted to the Royal London Hospital where doctors put me on traction and said they might have to amputate my leg. Thankfully they managed to repair it, but it forced me to be at home.

I asked Lev if it had been a fear of letting go that had forced him to try and do everything.

Definitely, it was a fear of losing the business. I looked at it as my baby. I have changed the whole way I think; I am letting the business take its own course now. Every time I go into hospital, I get time to think and have decided that I can't let it run my life. I am putting even less time into the business and it seems to be working for itself as it has doubled in size over the last year.

I asked Lev what his three key learnings had been.

1) Place trust in other people, but make sure you choose the right people in the first place. Look at their credentials. You wouldn't buy a bunch of bananas without checking if they are bruised first. Make sure you do your interviews right. Anyone can lie on a CV. I have to make sure, especially in my game, that they are right. Definitely don't rush into recruitment.

2) Don't be scared of subcontracting. It might even be to your competitor if you know they are good at what they do. It is sometimes good to build a relationship with another company.

3) You have to be tough from the beginning, but make sure you choose the right team.

Lev Fevzi, Smart Security Services www.sssuk.london

I thought this was such an inspiring story, not only in the way that Lev chose to see the accident as something positive, but because it is a great representation of how it is possible to create something bigger and more successful by getting out of the way. Lev simply had to let go, and by doing so he has more time and most importantly is enjoying life.

Chapter 7

GROWING SALES BEYOND THE BUILD SYSTEM

So far in the book we have worked our way through the BUILD system, which I designed purely to help Trades and Construction businesses create organisation. The BUILD system is for businesses in this sector which are experiencing an overwhelming demand for their services and are suffering from not being able to deal with it effectively. It is all about putting systems and processes in place, understanding who is best doing what and developing and retaining staff. If you have implemented the things we have discussed, I hope you are already starting to reap the benefits.

Once structures and routines are in place, things can change quite dramatically in a good way for the business owner. As you deal with all enquiries promptly and give your clients exceptional service, over time you will find that you are in the top 20% of your sector. Once this happens, your clients in effect become your marketing, as people are raving about you.

I have written this chapter to help business owners who have now got their house in order and have more time to focus on increasing sales. Because this is what happens when you have motivated people and the right systems in place: you suddenly find you have time on your hands.

I am going to take you through three key strategies to grow your sales which, when implemented together, can be very effective indeed.

USPs

How is what you do different to everyone else? Also known as your unique selling proposition (USP). Unless you have this clearly defined, you will always be seen as just another gas engineer, plumber, electrician, etc.

This is worth giving some thought to. More often than not when I ask someone what their USP is, they say great customer service, friendly staff, etc., etc. I'm afraid that this is not a USP.

Examples of USPs could be:

- Guaranteed visit within 24 hours for non-emergency call outs
- Quotes provided within 24 hours of visit
- Customer surveys report 95%+ of our customers are happy to recommend us
- Text messages are sent advising customers of estimated time of arrival (ETA)
- Dedicated help desk to answer customer queries

Anything that sets you apart as doing business in a better, more efficient and friendlier way than your competitors, providing that is what is happening in reality, will make you more attractive to customers.

Partnerships

By this I don't mean that you are going to go into business with someone else. Rather, think of this as partnering with them. Working in partnership with another professional who services the same target market as you do but doesn't compete with you can be a great way of driving sales. You are effectively introducing business to each other.

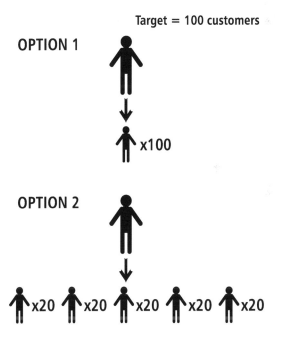

Target = 100 customers

OPTION 1

x100

OPTION 2

x20   x20   x20   x20   x20

The diagram above explains why partnerships are an efficient way of growing a business. Imagine that you need 100 customers next year in order to reach your financial targets. How many customers would you need to speak to? Not everyone you speak to will buy. It may only be one in three or four, but let's say that you are a very good salesperson and convert one in two. That would be 200 potential customers you would need to speak to in order to reach your target of 100.

Imagine now that you worked in partnership with five other professions in the Trades and Construction industries, e.g. you may be a plumber, and your partners could be an electrician, air conditioning installer, builder, roofer and tiler. They could all be introducers of business because they are working with your potential customers day in and day out, and those same customers are likely to need you at some time. Providing your partners do a good job, their customers will trust them. So when they recommend your services, customers are likely to go with their suggestion.

All you need to do is find the right five partners. If each of them passes 25 customers to you each year and you close 20 of them, you have reached your 100 target in a much more efficient way than you would on your own. Because there is a relationship involved with business that is passed via an introducing partner there is a stronger likelihood that you will win the business. What is more, you don't need to go out year after year looking for 100 new customers, because if you nurture and maintain good working relationships with your partners, they will keep giving you a steady stream of business.

There is a fundamental aspect to making the above work, and that is you first need to give in order to receive. If you put effort into finding business for the right partners, you will receive business in return. This is because it is natural to feel indebted to someone if they do something for us. So we have to train our brains to look out for opportunities for others rather than thinking about ourselves. Trust me, it will be far more enjoyable, and you will get more business in return.

How do you know if someone is going to be a good partner or not? Here are some things to look out for:

Is their company image professional? If they look smart, have a decent looking website, their van is sign written and they appear to be organised, you will definitely be on the right path.

Do they do what they say they will do? We tend to form judgments about others by how consistent their words and actions are. If someone says that they will get back to you or call you at a certain time and they don't, this will affect how you perceive them, whether it is conscious or not.

Do they appear to be organised? This is crucial because if they are not organised, the likelihood is that their customers won't be getting a good service. They probably won't be thinking of you when they are with a customer either, as they are likely to be fire-fighting most of the time.

Do they carry out high quality of work? This may be difficult to assess if their profession is not closely linked to yours, but you could ask to see customer testimonials.

Are they polite and courteous? Manners maketh man, and they are something that we tend to judge people on very quickly. It may bear no relevance to how good their standard of work is, but customers do form impressions by how professional and courteous a person is.

You want the answer to be yes in all the above cases if you are to be recommending your partners to your customers, otherwise it could reflect badly on you.

When thinking about which professions to partner with, consider two crucial factors. Firstly, which professions are you most likely to be able to refer business to? If you are a plumber, a tiler is a good example, because if you are installing a bathroom, the tiles will need to be replaced. If you are a builder, it may be a roofer or an electrician that you can work most closely with. If you are the electrician, it may be a plasterer.

Think also about which professions could refer to you. Essentially both professions need to be able to pass business between each other for this strategy to work well. It is the classic 'I'll scratch your back and you scratch mine' scenario.

I would focus on having three key professions to partner with, and a maximum of five. In terms of finding them and bringing them on board, I recommend that you treat this like a job vacancy. You want to find the right person and only one of them. This creates an element of scarcity, and the right type of person will get this and strive to be the chosen one.

I remember a few years back I applied this strategy to my business. I was looking to work with one, and only one, recruitment agency. I wanted it to be local and to specialise in small businesses.

I asked for introductions to recruitment agencies in my BNI group (see more about this later in the chapter), and I was given 24 referrals. This enabled me to call each one and explain that I was looking to form a working relationship with a recruitment agency as my clients were often in need of help to fill vacancies. Crucially I wasn't asking anything of them; in fact, it was the opposite. I was looking to give them business.

I ended up meeting with about five of the twenty-four. Some just didn't get the concept of what I was offering at all, so they were easily weeded out. I found an ideal local agency that I still pass business to today, and I receive business from them.

Once you have your list of professions, there are several ways in which to find them:

LinkedIn. By searching for certain professions using the search box, you can see who is connected to you through someone you know. You will know who they are as they will have a small 2nd in the top right hand corner of their profile. This means that both of you have a 1st degree connection in common. If you ask your 1st degree connection to introduce you, they will be far more open to speaking to you.

Google. You could search for 'electrician Bromley' and contact a few that come up in the search – firstly checking out their website and reviews, of course.

Checkatrade, Trust a Trader, *Which* – all of these can be great ways of checking out how good people are at what they do.

Word of mouth. This is perhaps the best starting place as those who are recommended by your network are probably the safest of bets. Again you're asking someone you both know to introduce you.

Networking groups. The one that I would personally recommend is BNI, purely because it is not really a networking group but a referral organisation. There are key differences, and I go into this in a lot more detail further on in this chapter.

The key here is to remember the psychology. As we say in BNI, 'givers gain.' In other words, the language you use must be all about what is in it for your potential partners as opposed to what is in it for you. Don't worry, the right people get this and will give you business in return.

This is a suggested script:

> *Hi there, my name is XXXX and I run a local electrical installation business based in XXXXX. We are looking for a quality plasterer to pass business to as we often find that our clients don't have anyone they can trust, and we want to provide as much of a one stop shop service for them as we can without doing this element of the work ourselves. We are only looking to work with one plasterer in the local area so that we can build a good working relationship. Would you be interested in meeting for a coffee to discuss?*

If the people you approach appear as though they don't really understand the concept, politely leave it. It's not worth the trouble; move on to the next one. You are looking for positive, driven and professional individuals. If the person appears negative at this stage, you can imagine what they will be like further down the line, and what they may be like with customers.

Networking

There are several networking groups that tradespeople can join, as well as one-off events. Being part of a group enables you to build relationships, and therefore trust, with other business owners. This can be a very powerful way of building your brand in the local area, as many people prefer to ask their friends for recommendations rather than google a particular service.

BNI. I can strongly recommend BNI www.bni.com. If you join a BNI Chapter, the group effectively becomes your sales team as there is an expectation for each member to bring business. Chapters meet every week and the amount of business being passed is tracked, in effect making each Chapter like a mini business of its own.

BNI can be like Marmite – there are plenty of people out there who hate it as well as love it. This can often be down to someone having a bad experience, and word gets around.

For a Trades or Construction business, BNI is an absolute no-brainer. In fact, if you are lucky enough to be accepted into a Chapter, get ready to grow quickly. You will effectively be taking the partnership strategy and applying it within a group of people who meet every week.

Each Chapter only allows one of each profession to join, which effectively locks out your competition. I joined a local Chapter as a business coach – a category that can sometimes struggle because it is not always clear what a business coach does – eight months after starting my business, and have never looked back. A plumber, electrician, builder, scaffolder, roofer, etc. can therefore get business very quickly, providing they put time in to building relationships with the others in the group.

The psychology behind making something like this work is exactly the same as making partnerships work. The beauty with BNI is that whomever you are looking for an introduction to, the probability is that someone in your Chapter will know them, especially if they are local. We are no longer separated by seven degrees; nowadays it is more like three degrees. So many times I meet someone (anywhere in the world) then enter them into LinkedIn and find that they are somewhere in my network.

There is a well-known story that is often circulated around our region within BNI about a guy who had a business that built treehouses for children. He had read somewhere that Elton John and his husband David Furnish wanted to have a treehouse built for their son. He therefore asked at his BNI meeting a few times for an introduction to Elton John and explained why, raising a few chuckles in the room.

He was on holiday with his family and the phone rang. The person calling said they were representing Elton John. They had been given this guy's details as they had been told he built amazing treehouses. Even though he thought it was a wind-up, he went along with it, and just as well he did, because it was genuine. He ended up building the most amazing treehouse for Elton and David's son.

This is the power of a referral organisation such as BNI, but it also shows the power of asking for what you want. If you want to work with a particular sector of the market, then say this. The more specific you can be, the more your ideal customers will show up.

I interviewed Charlie Lawson, the National Director of BNI.

What would you say to any Trades business considering joining BNI?

I would want to know that they want to grow a business. One of the biggest challenges Trades find is that they want work, but the way BNI works, they are then inundated and have to step away. They need to want to grow and expand and take on people.

What advice would you give to them if they were accepted?

Follow the system – it works. It has been proven over many years, and thousands of groups. Networking isn't a quick fix; it takes time to build relationships, especially if you are dealing in bigger jobs.

A great example is a decorator in Scotland. The first referral he got was to paint the bottom of an office door – that same client asked him to come back and do some touching up, then radiators. All tiny jobs, but he did them well, built the credibility and then he got the whole office.

How would you say BNI differs from other networking groups?

It differs because it is about the accountability and the fact we track everything that goes on. The committee looks at everything that happens. You are expected to give something, but unless you have this accountability, nothing happens. The accountability from everyone in the group makes it work. Every piece of business gets tracked.

What key things make it work?

I think it's the relationships we build. You can't refer a contact unless you know they are going to do a good job. The relationships have to be there, but sometimes you don't then want to hold people accountable. The best groups hold each other accountable and have great relationships, which means you are going to get the results.

What are some things you see tradespeople doing in BNI that make it unsuccessful for them?

If they are just looking to fill their 9–5, it won't work for them. In fact, it could damage them as they will be stretched and won't be successful because they aren't looking to grow.

What are some things you see tradespeople doing in BNI that make it successful for them?

One of the most successful was a roofing company. The business owner wasn't right for BNI at all. Public speaking, finding referrals wasn't his cup of tea. His partner who looked after the office, however, was superb, and therefore they became the member. This is something that tradespeople often overlook – it doesn't have to be the owner joining. Don't disregard it if networking isn't your thing; it might be better for someone else to do it.

So now you have loads of ideas and strategies to continue to build and grow your business.

In summary, identify some key professions that could yield partners. Approach people, remembering to use language that is focused on helping them, not asking them for something. Visit your local BNI Chapter or another networking group. Most importantly, continue to refer back to the BUILD system to ensure that you maintain strong foundations to support continued growth.

SUMMARY

I really hope that you have found this book insightful, practical and useful. The BUILD system has been proven to work with several business sectors, but has produced the best results with businesses that have an overwhelming demand for their services, as Trades often do.

If you are an ambitious owner of a Trades business and have aspirations to grow, use this book as a reference tool, and keep referring back to the parts that are most relevant to you at any given time.

The key points we have covered are:

Know where you are going and have a plan of how to get there. Ensure that you take time out to think about where you would like to be three years, two years and one year from now.

Often when I ask people where they would like to be in three years in terms of the business, I can guess what is going through their mind. Their face says it all: 'Yeah, I wish' and 'As if', but when you set big goals and break these down into how many additional customers they equate to, often you can see how achievable it all is.

Running a business is very much like playing a game. You just need to know the rules and plan ahead. It is amazing to see how light bulbs go on in people's minds when they realise all they need to do is set some stretching goals and take small steps towards them.

Someone once said to me that if you plan to hike to the top of a mountain, you would never set off if you set your goal as the top. It would seem too much of a challenge, and the little voice in your head would be telling you it is impossible to climb that far. However, if you set smaller milestones along the way and celebrate them, suddenly the top of the mountain doesn't seem so far out of reach.

Jacques from JP Air Conditioning says of the plan he implemented:

> It's very exciting to see where my business is going. I track my business every month, and I will reach my goal before the year-end. It's amazing how many clients we get on a daily basis. I would put this down to customer service because the office systems are in place to deal with enquiries the same day they come in.

Know your numbers. It is simply not good enough to run a business without knowing your key numbers. In fact, I would say you aren't actually running a business if you don't know them. Rather you are an employee in your own business, and one who doesn't know how the company is doing.

Hopefully you have grasped from this book that the numbers side of the business should be delegated to someone, but this doesn't mean that you can abdicate yourself from responsibility. Set aside time each week to review the numbers. This will ensure that you are more likely to make the right decisions, and can effectively plan ahead.

Make sure that you review Key Performance Indicators (KPIs) which are the numbers on your monthly profit and loss accounts, e.g. sales, expenses and profit, and compare them to your forecast. KPIs show you how successful you have been, but cannot be changed. This is why every business should also have a set of three to five critical indicators which are your traffic lights. These alert you to a problem in time for you to react and take action.

Surround yourself with people who love doing the things you hate. All of us have our own strengths and weaknesses. We are all different, which makes the world interesting. The problem is that we are brought up in an education system that encourages us to ignore our strengths and focuses us on 'fixing' our weaknesses. This approach will only ever produce mediocre results, as there is no such thing as a good all-rounder.

The approach I have explained in this book flips this on its head. I am giving you permission to focus on what comes naturally to you, so if this is getting out there and seeing customers, winning the business, go and do it. Or if you are creative and are great at designing structures, do this. But you will need to let go of the things that you may have been trying all your life to fix, e.g. the admin, the invoicing, the preparing of quotes, etc.

Of course this is only successful if you find the right person whose strengths are your weaknesses. So invest time in planning out what you need, advertise the role so you have plenty of people to choose from, telephone interview, consider psychometric testing and ensure you conduct a competency based interview face to face. Your hit rate will go through the roof.

Kris Jamroz from Brush Strokes says:

> *Find people you can trust by having a system in place to identify them. Having the right people made it [delegation] a lot easier.*

Ensure the left hand knows what the right hand is doing. In order for a lot of things to be realised, you need to be organised. If you make sure staff are set clear expectations, they are more likely to perform well. If you hold regular meetings, the team will feel well informed, and templates such as a GANTT chart will track and measure projects. Then everyone is much more likely to know what is required and how they are doing against target.

Stay in the top 20% and save on marketing. The better the service you provide, the more people will recommend you to friends and family. Word soon gets around how good, or bad, the local electrician, plumber or builder is, and this of course can work against as well as for you. It is hard to get a good reputation, but easy to get a bad one. Because the Trades and Construction industries do not generally have the best reputation when it comes to customer service, you have a real opportunity to stand out from the crowd if you get it right and keep it that way.

Recruit, develop and retain. This is probably the hardest element to get right. Finding good people and keeping them is difficult for most businesses, regardless of the sector. Spend quality time on the recruitment and selection process, time with your staff developing and appraising them, and time communicating with them regularly. This will pay dividends in the long run.

Often I hear, 'I just don't have the time'. I would say have the courage to make the time, and it will pay off. You will have fewer problems, fewer headaches and more time to focus on the fun elements of your business, like getting more customers.

Here is what Kris from Brush Strokes had to say when I asked him how he had implemented some of the people processes into his business:

If you try and sit with a painter and a form, it doesn't work. I go on site, there are down times, and we sit over a coffee, looking at problems. I have a little bit of time with the painter, thinking about what is on the form, having a chat. Because they are the right people, I have listening ears. So it was about adapting office procedures and making them work for a site environment.

I truly hope that this book has been enlightening for you and has developed some untapped potential within your business. My aim is to help Construction and Trades business owners be the best they can be and create an enriching, stress-free life that they previously may have thought was impossible. Parts of the book which didn't resonate the first time may well the second or third time you read them. As your business moves on, what was not relevant before may become so.

It astounds me the amount of untapped potential there is in many businesses and people, especially within Construction and Trades. There is no other sector I can think of that has such an ability to grow and grow quickly, providing the right foundations are in place – if you'll excuse the pun!

As Abraham Lincoln famously said, 'The best way to predict the future is to create it', so with this knowledge, go and do just that.

INTERVIEW WITH CHARLIE MULLINS OBE, FOUNDER AND CHAIRMAN OF PIMLICO PLUMBERS

Pimlico Plumbers is arguably the most successful and well-known plumbing business in the world. Charlie Mullins, OBE founded it in 1979 and today it has 350 plumbers as part of its workforce.

Charlie is a most interesting character, clearly a stickler for attention to detail and standards. What interested me when I met him is that he has implemented many processes that you would find within a corporate environment, initiatives that often don't live and breathe as they are intended to in those companies, but within Pimlico Plumbers I could see that they do, and it appeared to me to be a very good place to work.

I have included below his top tips on what he believes has made Pimlico Plumbers the business that it is today:

1. *If you want to grow you have to employ people and the right people. We drew up a book called the Pimlico bible... what we want from somebody – rules and regulations, dress like this, behave like this, we start at this time, we have clean vans... the successful way to run a business. If you've got this then everyone is drinking from the same teapot. It's your terms of business.*

Any business is only as good as the people it employs, undoubtedly it is about finding the right people... the better people are in place because the systems are in place.

Until you employ people you can only earn one man's money.'

2. You have to delegate and learn to trust people. *The biggest challenge I found was delegating and trusting people and realising that I can't do everything, I'm not good at everything.'*

3. Make sure you surround yourself with people who are good at the things you aren't. *You have to realise what you are good at and surround yourself with others who are good at other things. I started to put the right pegs in the right holes... the art of it is getting the right people, believing in them and letting them get on with the job'*

4. Have high standards. *We set our standards high, we don't put up with scruffy or late people. We work for top clients, charge top rates and they expect top service. In the early days, it was about saying the same message and eventually it filters through, it becomes second nature.*

We have got quality control managers now who look for what people aren't doing right. It says on the website the type of people we employ. Our reputation is high and people are aware of it.

5. Have an operating structure in place. *When we nearly went bust years ago we had no structure. I am a great believer in managers, everywhere you go there is a manager. I learnt to delegate; at some stage you have to remember you can't do everything.*

In the recession of 1990 we nearly went bust. I went from being the best thing since sliced bread to the worst businessman, overnight. My accountant was telling me we had no structure – I didn't know what structure I needed. I was involved with the wages, this that and the other. You have got to have other people. It was all coming on to me – maybe it was my mistake, I was trying to do everything.

6. Cash flow is so important. *The other learning was giving people credit, so many people go out of business because someone else owes them money, so changing our terms and conditions (was a learning), we went from invoicing to payment on completion.*

Use staged payments, deposits. So many people say if I don't give them credit someone else will; well, let them go out of business.

Cash flow is so important – my learning curve was the recession and credit control, if you haven't got that side of it right you are going to go bust.

7. Do the opposite of what customers hate. *I came up with a list of all the things people don't like about plumbers, e.g. being scruffy, guessing prices, leaving the job half way through etc, and we did the opposite. It wasn't that Pimlico Plumbers were so clever, it's just that the others were so bad!*

We all know what the bad things are in your industry: just do the opposite.

8. Measure the service. *Follow up: what really makes Pimlico Plumbers is the quality of service we provide from the phone call to the plumber to the after care, whether it is trades people or a product. People will always pay for quality.*

We have Quality Control Managers; their job is to check with the engineers and check with the customers.

Quite often, after-sales calls create a bit more work. All of a sudden you have someone else ringing up to check how things are. Of 2000 jobs a week, between 70–80% are return customers. We work on the basis that we hope you are a Pimlico Plumber customer for life. We got through the last recession because of our existing customers.

If you are brave enough find out if they don't like you and try and rectify it.

I asked Charlie what his advice would be to someone who wasn't sure about taking the leap and growing their business. It was quite simple:

Do it gradually, the benefits are chalk and cheese. If you get it right there is nothing like having your own business. The plus side of it outweighs the sleepless nights; financially the rewards are there, as is the satisfaction.

ACKNOWLEDGEMENTS

I would like to thank:

My parents Geoff and Dorothy for developing my ability to budget, a life-skill which has underpinned much of my success in business.

My partner Mike for all his encouragement and support.

The inspirational managers I have worked for and alongside in organisations, in particular Steven Davis, Gordon Lyle, John Estill and Howard Schultz.

James Brook and Dr Paul Brewerton of Strengths Partnership Ltd for introducing me to the Strengths philosophy.

My business mentors who I have learnt so much from over the last few years: Dan Bradbury, Nick James, Roger James Hamilton, Daniel Priestley and Andrew Priestley.

The team at Rethink Press, in particular Lucy McCarraher and Joe Gregory for their valuable guidance and support in writing this book.

Charlie Mullins OBE, Founder and Chairman of Pimlico Plumbers for his generosity and ongoing support.

Claire Byrne ACMA, Head of Finance, Checkatrade.com for her invaluable contribution.

BNI Churchill: this networking group has been instrumental in allowing me to grow both my business and personally, over the last seven years.

My assistant Kathleen McCord for her wonderful attention to detail and ongoing support, and my fabulous team Jennie, Katie, Sue, Reyhana and Emma.

My amazing clients, who I continue to learn from each day. In particular I would like to thank those clients who were generous enough to share their journeys in this book so that they may inspire others: Lee Sadler, Mark Lydon, Jacques Pretorius, Roland Nagy, Rob Aitken and Kris Jamroz.

Other business owners who were equally generous in sharing their insights for the book: Esther Fagbemiro, Tony Hawkes, Charlie Lawson and Lev Fevzi.

Denise Tiran, Neil Gulvin, Maggie Pretorius, Kris, Lee and Claire for providing such valuable feedback on the book in its test stage.

Finally, I would like to recognise all the hard working trade business owners who strive to be the best they can be. I hope this book has inspired you to predict and create your future.

THE AUTHOR

 Alison Warner is the Founder of Evolve and Grow Ltd, a business coaching and consultancy firm based in London, UK. Her passion is in developing untapped potential in both people and businesses.

Alison's background consists of working for some of the world's most recognisable brands within Retail and Hospitality. She was an Area Manager for a number of years, where she was utilised as a trouble-shooter, going into areas that were under-performing to turn them around.

Alison looked after Resourcing for a high-end coffee chain in the UK and Ireland during a period of rapid growth for the company at a time when they were opening three stores a week. She was awarded Leader of the Year in 2008 for the systems and processes she had implemented and the team she had developed to support this growth.

In 2010 she founded Evolve and Grow and began working with many SMEs, quickly realising that the sector that had the most untapped potential was Construction and Trades. Her client base includes plumbers, electricians, glaziers, builders, air-conditioning, gardeners, painters and decorators and window cleaners.

It is the same systems and processes that she used within large organisations that have helped her create the BUILD system, a 5-step process that helps Construction and Trade business owners with an annual turnover of £100-300k move off the tools and into a position where they can grow their business.

In 2016, Alison launched 'Build and Grow', a range of one-on-one 6-month business development programmes created around the BUILD system, specifically to support ambitious owners of trade businesses.

In 2017 she won Key Person of Influence 'Pitchfest'.

You can contact Alison via:

Website: www.evolveandgrowcoaching.com
Facebook: https://www.facebook.com/tradesandbuilders/
Twitter: @evolveandgrow
LinkedIn: https://www.linkedin.com/in/alisonwarner1/

Printed in Great Britain
by Amazon